Emily Murphy: Rebel

Emily Ferguson Murphy

First Female Magistrate
in the British Empire

Emily Murphy: Rebel

Christine Mander

Simon & Pierre
TORONTO, CANADA

We would like to express our gratitude to The Canada Council and the Ontario Arts Council for their support.

Marian M. Wilson, Publisher

ISBN 0-88924-173-2

1 2 3 4 5 • 9 8 7 6 5

Canadian Cataloguing in Publication Data

Mander, Christine.
Emily Murphy, rebel

Bibliography: p.
Includes index.
ISBN 0-88924-173-2

1. Murphy, Emily F. (Emily Ferguson), 1868-1933. 2. Women judges - Canada - Biography. 3. Feminists - Canada - Biography. 4. Women authors, Canadian (English) - Biography.* 5. Women's rights - Canada - History. 6. Women - Legal status, laws, etc. - Canada - History. I. Title.

KE411.M87M35 1985   342.71'0878'0924   C85-099680-5

General Editor: Marian M. Wilson
Editor: Sarah Robertson
Assistant Editor: Jean Paton
Typesetting & Design: Cundari Group Ltd.
Printer: Imprimerie Gagne Ltée.
Printed and Bound in Canada

Order From
Simon & Pierre Publishing Company Limited
P.O. Box 280 Adelaide Street Postal Station
Toronto, Ontario, Canada M5C 2J4

To Ron

Other Books by Christine Mander

All You Need Is Enough Rope: A lighthearted look at cottage life.
Hamilton: Potlatch Publications, 1981

Contents

Illustrations

All pictures not otherwise credited are from private collections.

Acknowledgements

For her gracious permission to use material from her mother's excellent biography, *Emily Murphy: Crusader,* I owe a debt of gratitude to Dodie Finlayson of Massachusetts, as I do for their help and patience through the rough and the smooth, to Helen LaRose and her staff at the Edmonton City Archives.

In carrying out research for this book, I had two strokes of good fortune. The first was to learn of the CBC Radio Classified program, a free service which is broadcast twice weekly out of Toronto. This led directly to the second piece of luck, meeting Emily's niece, Miss Maude Murphy, whose reminiscences, and willingness to rummage through family papers and albums earned my gratitude. To her, and to her sister, Vi Penney, who also helped—my very sincere thanks.

To Lotta Dempsey for reminiscences, Joan McLean of the Cookstown Historical and Heritage Society for leads, and Daniel Webster, rector's warden at St. John's Anglican Church, Cookstown, for checking old records—my thanks.

The City of Edmonton Police Department suggested leads which proved fruitful, and the British Tourist Authority (Toronto) came through with some London addresses which I needed.

Alberta Government departments went out of their way to be helpful, and I am particularly grateful to the Department of Vital Statistics, which parted some red tape to confirm cause of death, when all other sources were speculative. ACCESS (Alberta Educational Communications Corporation) in Edmonton, very kindly allowed me to preview its film, *The Persons Case,* and the Canada Council Explorations Grant went a long way to getting the book started.

Researching is, by and large, a fairly plodding task, but occasionally new leads to old facts emerge as little triumphs along the way. Earning my thanks under this heading are Dr. John Hastings of Toronto, an authority on the Gowan family, who came to my rescue on several occasions, through the good auspices of Elaine and Betty Hall who put us in touch, and the Upper Canada Railroad Society of Toronto, to whom I would unfailingly go in future for information on train travel in bygone days.

Just when I was wondering how to move heaven and earth to obtain a seemingly unobtainable photograph from the Royal Ontario Museum, director Dr. J.E. Cruise, leapt into the breach earning my gratitude, and Jennifer Hamblin of the Glenbow Museum made some useful suggestions which moved things along.

Who could do without librarians at a time like this? My thanks to the National Library, Ottawa, and the Hamilton (Ontario) Public Library for their speedy Interlibrary Loan Service; the *Toronto Star* Library; and the Rare books libraries at the Universities of Waterloo, Calgary, McMaster, Alberta, Toronto (Rachel Grover of Thomas Fisher Rare Books Library, U. of T.—hello!), and the Law Library in Edmonton, my thanks for your assistance.

Finally, to the reference staff at the Oakville Public Library in my home town, who may be forgiven for thinking I had no home to go to, my special appreciation for their unflagging help, expertise and interest.

Christine Mander

Foreword

Emily Murphy is a woman for all seasons. I say "is" because I hope, through this book, to keep the spirit of "Janey Canuck" alive—that same spirit which Byrne Hope Sanders introduced to the world in her biography many years ago.

Emily had no qualms about her place in the world, no problem identifying her aims, and above all no reticence about communicating her strong beliefs and cogent sense of responsibility to her fellow men and women.

She was a believer in action; she was persuasive with words; she was a force to be reckoned with in whatever task she undertook, whether it was singing a child to sleep, being a helpmate to her husband, or a hellion on the hustings. Her philosophy on how a woman should best tackle life was characterized by a strong thread of honest-to-goodness common sense which is as apt for the computer age as it was for the "Votes for Women" one in which she grew up.

As far as I could, I have let Emily tell you her story in her own words. She was certainly eloquent enough. If, in consequence, more people—men and women—are encouraged to listen, we shall all be well rewarded.

Prologue

"To Hell with Women Magistrates"

The best way to destroy enemies is to make friends of them. If you get quite near a person his blow loses its force. The same applies to the kick of a mule... Stand by, then, and stand close.

On Thursday, 25th October 1917, a letter arrived at the Edmonton offices of E.E.A.H. Jackson Esq., Messrs. Cormack, MacKie & Van Allen, Barristers.

Sir,

I am informed this morning in the Women's Police Court at the conclusion of the case of Rex v Nora Holt, you, in the presence of several persons, made use of the following grossly insulting words:

> *"To Hell with Women Magistrates. This country is going to the dogs because of them. I would commit suicide before I would pass a sentence like that."*

Unless I receive from you an unqualified apology in writing, I shall regretfully be obliged to henceforth refuse you admittance to this Court in the capacity of Counsel.

> *I have the honour to be, Sir,*
> *Your obedient servant,*
> *Emily F. Murphy*
> Police Magistrate for the City of Edmonton.[1]

Emily Ferguson Murphy, the first woman to be appointed Police Magistrate in the British Empire, was tired of Mr. Eardley Jackson and his insults. If he wanted a fight, he'd got one. Her appointment to the Bench had happened very suddenly. One midsummer day in 1916 two members of the local Council of Women in Edmonton had come to her for advice. They had been sent by their law committee to witness the trial of a group of prostitutes who had been rounded up under suspicious circumstances that might have contravened the law. Expected to report back, the women were flummoxed by the counsel for the Crown's request that they leave the court: they might hear what was not fit for their ears.

In those days, women were not expected to interest themselves in the more sordid aspects of life. In the eyes of society, there were "ladies," who sang or sewed—and "other females," who did not. Society liked its women to be simple, easily definable, and so the law, a masculine domain, slammed down a hard fist on the unwed mother, the young girl from a broken home forced to make a living on the street, as well as the seasoned prostitute. "Other females" were disposable items, put out of the way with a "six months hard labour" and a bang of the gavel.

The questionable rights of women and children were, however, being examined and challenged by women's groups. Fed up with being told by crown prosecutors that the evidence heard in police courts was "not fit for mixed company," they wanted action—and change. Hence the visit to Emily Murphy, already renowned for her championing of the persecuted.

Emily was typically forthright. "If the evidence is not fit to be heard in mixed company," she said, "then you must lobby the government to set up a special court presided over by women, to try other women." It was a simple but revolutionary solution. The Council of Women liked it, and appealed to Emily to be their spokeswoman.

Emily protested. Busy with her own affairs, she had no desire to become embroiled in what she felt was something the women themselves should handle.

"But, Mrs. Murphy, you're so *good* at this sort of thing," they implored.

A few days later Emily Murphy presented herself at the office of the Honorable Charles W. Cross, expecting, and prepared for, considerable resistance. She put forward her recommendation to the Attorney General in as forceful a tone as she could muster—and was completely taken aback when he agreed that a special court was needed.

"The Governor-General meets next week," he said, "could you be ready, Mrs. Murphy, to be sworn in as Police Magistrate, if the idea is ratified?"

Emily was dumbfounded by this turn of events. How had she got herself into this situation anyway? How could she get herself out of it? For once, caught off balance, she found herself stammering her unreadiness, her ignorance of the law, her work, her family.

"I...I just never thought of this," she gasped, finally.

The Attorney General smiled. "Let me know in a week," he replied. Emily fled.

It took considerable persuasion from her proud family—and assurances of legal aid from her brothers—before she relented, but on June 19, 1916, vivacious, fun-loving Emily Murphy, devoted wife and mother, a woman already known far and wide as author and roving reporter "Janey Canuck," became, in her forty-eighth year, Magistrate Murphy, civic leader, controversial public figure, and battler for human rights.

While the appointment was hailed by many, it was met with something less than enthusiasm by male officers of the courts who had made a significant discovery: a woman was not a "person" under the British North America Act of 1867.[2] Emily, who had overcome her initial apprehensions at taking the job, took this in stride too, but she inwardly fumed at the injustice of it. Incidents such as the "To Hell" speech of Eardley Jackson made her anger boil over. When her counterpart in Calgary, Alice J. Jamieson, whose magisterial appointment had followed her own by several months, received similar treatment, the issue went all the way up to the Supreme Court of Alberta, and Emily watched the proceedings closely.

In one of her cases, Magistrate Jamieson had failed to solicit evidence from the accused before passing sentence, a not unheard-of oversight; the defence had already presented its case, and Magistrate Jamieson had offered to rectify matters then and there. Defence counsel, however, seizing the opportunity to challenge the magistrate's status, applied to have the sentence quashed. When this was dismissed, he appealed the decision to the Supreme Court on the grounds that the magistrate "...being a woman, is incompetent and incapable of holding the appointment of Police Magistrate."[3]

The following November the Alberta Supreme Court declared its finding that "...in this province and at this time...there is at common law no legal disqualification for holding public office in the government of the country arising from any distinction of sex..." It was a signal victory. But to Emily it was only a beginning. That women's status should continue to depend upon the interpretation of an outdated and outmoded law was unthinkable. The law itself had to be changed, and she vowed to do it.

First Alberta, then the nation!

It was an uphill fight which took her twelve years, culminating in the famous Persons Case of 1929, when the Privy Council at Westminster, on October 18th, gave final recognition to women as "persons," thus acknowledging their right to hold the highest public office in the land. Four years later, she had the additional satisfaction of hearing a transformed Eardley Jackson refer to her as "this beloved lady."

That was Emily Ferguson Murphy for you. Born a fighter, died a fighter. As she was often heard to say: "The world loves a peaceful man, but gives way to a strenuous kicker."

Chapter I

Growing up in Cookstown: 1868-1882

If a woman be called upon to write of those dream-sweet hours when, as a child, life was a riddle yet unread, ah, the task is a hard one, and stubborn to the pen.

Confederation was barely eight months old when Emily Ferguson was born on March 14, 1868 in the little village of Cookstown, Ontario, the third child and first daughter of Isaac and Emily (Gowan) Ferguson.

"The Ferguson Place," as it was known to Cookstown's two hundred or so families, stood back off the road in a grove of maple trees, as befitted the house of a well-to-do landowner and businessman. Isaac Ferguson had done well for himself since arriving in Canada in 1842, a fatherless boy of twelve. His father, Andrew, had died at sea on the way over from Co. Cavan, Ireland, with the family, but his young wife, Mary Ann (Roberts), Isaac's mother, with her six children carried out the plans he had made, and settled in Simcoe County. There, Isaac, the youngest son, grew up and prospered, eventually marrying the youngest daughter of Ogle Robert Gowan, a wealthy politician. The granddaughter never knew her grandmother, for Mary Ann died when Emily was in her first year.

The Gowans played their part in Ireland's turbulent and bloody history. Involved in the 1798 Rebellion was the notorious magistrate Hunter Gowan of Mount Nebo in the county of Wexford, a *pied noir* who had started life as a professional outlaw hunter and later became leader of an irregular group of Protestants roaming the country in search of rebels. This gang, the "Black Mob," with a few other loyalists, enrolled in some of the first unofficial Orange Lodge groups to spring up since the foundation of the official Orange Order in Ireland in 1795.[1]

Several decades later, Ogle Robert Gowan, Emily's grandfather, arrived in Canada with his household of nine and bought Escott Park, an estate of four hundred acres near Brockville, Ontario. A confirmed Orangeman, he obtained a warrant from the English Lodge to establish a formal Grand Lodge in Canada, and became its first Deputy Grand Master in 1830. Some years later in Brockville, in 1837, his wife, Frances Anne (Colclough-Turner) designed the flag bearing the inscription, "Down with Elgin and his rebel-paying Ministry." It was hoisted on the lakefront during the visit of Lord

*Frances Anne Colclough-Turner, Emily Murphy's
maternal grandmother*

Elgin, and has ever since been called "Mrs. Gowan's Petticoat." The
Rebellion Losses Bill, which gave compensation for losses suffered as a
result of the Mackenzie Rebellion in 1837, angered the Orangemen who
did not see why some of the Rebels should, as they felt, benefit from their
treachery.[2]

Ogle Gowan went into politics and became known as "Father of the
House" because of his twenty-seven years of service. By some he was also
known as "Father of the Press" because he worked with newspapers (some
of which he owned) to fight for the Unity of Canada and its allegiance
to the British Empire. After his death in 1876, Ogle Gowan's memory was
kept alive by an annual tribute paid to his daughter, in the form of songs,
drums and pipes played and sung by the Cookstown Orange Band. This
glorious affair (referred to by "Mother Gibson," the housekeeper, as "The
Annyual"), was attended by small boys, lusty adolescents, assorted
townsfolk and their dogs. Up the road, round the corner, and into the
Ferguson garden they trooped, where jars of orange lilies had been placed
for the occasion. Lights streamed across the croquet lawns, as Emily
Gowan Ferguson, on her husband's arm, welcomed the revellers into the
house with stacks of sandwiches and cauldrons of hot coffee.

Blue-eyed, black-haired Isaac Ferguson was a man of strong positive
qualities. ("God's hand did not tremble when He made this father of

mine.") He believed in equal sharing of responsibilities between his sons and daughters, but drew the line at whipping the girls for misdemeanors. The assigned place for this punishment was the little room off the dining room, and who knows what tortures little Emily went through as her brothers were unceremoniously marched off to pay for the latest mischief in which she, too, had been a willing participant. It is fair to assume, however, that the boys made the most of the situation and took every opportunity to play upon their sister's sympathies to the hilt.

Isaac Ferguson in 1880

Emily's recollections of her mother are of a woman with large, widely spaced eyes and hair parted in the middle, worn coronet-shaped about her head. Mrs. Ferguson was perfectly content being a jewel in her husband's crown, with no thought or desire for any kind of pursuit of her own. Emily also remembered her gentleness, the flower patterned dresses she wore — and how she always had about her the fragrance of violets. It was from her mother that she acquired her affinity for biblical stories and sayings: her ability to memorize them, almost word for word, was undoubtedly a product of the weekly recitations from the Anglican Book of Prayer which her mother conducted.

The Ferguson family religion was Church of England, but as there was no Anglican church in Cookstown at that time, the family worshipped at the local Methodist Church, where the rector sermonized at some length on the evils of card playing. Emily and Isaac were unmoved by the

Emily Gowan Ferguson

whisperings and meaningful glances sent their way by some of the congregation; they, and the many guests who joined them, continued to enjoy their games of whist, despite the scandalized twitterings of their Methodist neighbours.

In her book *Open Trails* (1912) Emily gives us a unique picture of the house where she was born, of growing up, and, incidentally, of Canadian social life at the turn of the century:

> It was an old-fashioned house of the style known as Colonial. The front door was panelled, and around it were little panes of glass. The dining room was our living room. It had windows set in deep casements, and always they were hung with green rep curtains drawn back by heavy, woollen cords that had tassels at the ends...
>
> The walls were wainscoted with some dark wood and, if we except the table, the biggest piece of furniture was a settle with high, curved ends and capable of seating all six of us at once. In keeping with the period, and the uses to which it was put, it was appropriately covered with horsehair. It was prime fun I can tell you, to take a header off the end of it and turn somersaults on the springs.

It was great fun, too, making the rounds of the glasses after guests had called, and consuming whatever dregs there were:

> I can remember clearly the niceties of the decanters, and how it was possible to gauge the guests by the decanter which was produced. Men on business were given malt whisky, either in its purity or, if the weather were cold, in the form of hot punch. Although he seldom drank with anyone, my father treated his especial friends to cherry punch or punch with lemon in it. Neither was it unusual to give this drink to ladies who had driven in from one of the neighbouring villages to spend the day with my mother. In this case, it was called "cherry cordial" and held to be a most excellent preventive against catching one's death of cold...
>
> We youngsters used to eat the cherries, lemon, and sugar out of the bottom of the tumblers, and so, according to all known precedent, should have turned out black sheep who, like the reformed temperance lecturers, "learned to love liquor at our father's table." But, strange to relate, none of us did....

And what temptations there were for a soul consumed with a penchant for play-acting! Besides a big, wooden chest full of old-fashioned finery—a dolman of watered silk, heavy with jet, a pelerine of velvet and lace, a blue silk dress with pendent bugles, veils and fans, and other accessories well calculated to excite the imagination of a little girl who wanted so desperately to be grown up — there was the parlor and the fatal mirror:

> The parlour was a long room with a square piano, plenty of pictures and books, and heavy, low furniture. There was also a large, plate glass mirror which rested on a marble stand near the floor. I used to pose before this, and pretend I was Rachel, the great actress. I do not know why I selected Rachel for my ideal, but possibly because I knew of no other. My last pose before it was on the eve of my wedding. On this occasion I placed a lamp on the stand that I might better see the draping of my bridal dress.
>
> The heat of the lamp cracked the mirror in quite fifty directions. My mother had it covered with curtains that the guests might not see, but the guests saw, and more than one woman looked at me with curious, half-frightened eyes. From that day till this nothing unfortunate has happened to me which has not been assigned to the breaking of that wretched mirror.

Emily's mother probably encouraged these daydreams for she, the youngest of the Gowans, was a beautiful, graceful woman who enjoyed to the full her life as hostess, entertaining her husband's business and political friends. She certainly did her best to discourage her daughter's proclivity for what she considered "unnatural" pursuits for a girl: tree climbing, fishing for suckers and sunfish and plotting to filch apples from a neighbor's orchards. Emily also played cricket, rode astride and took care of her own pony. One of her more acerbic comments later in life was about women and horseriding: "A girl who rides a horse sidewise looks like a heap of clothes hanging on a clothespeg, and likely to fall off at any minute."

Emily Murphy, aged 7. "There was a large, plate glass mirror...I used to pose before this, and pretend I was Rachel, the great actress."

William and Annie had already joined Emily and her older brothers, Thomas Roberts and Gowan. Harcourt completed the family circle when he was born after an interval of ten years in 1883.

A centre for many activities, the Murphy home became an integral part of the early political life of the province, especially through Ogle and his cousin Sir James Gowan, a Supreme Court Judge and eventual Senator. Uncle Thomas Roberts Ferguson married Emily Gowan's eldest sister Frances, and thus became a double relative. He was a colorful, very political figure, a huge man, known as "Fighting Tom." Cousin Justice Thomas Ferguson entertained them all on many eagerly anticipated occasions with stories of his cases; it is no wonder that, in this environment, three of the four Ferguson boys should seek their future careers in law, Tom and Harcourt becoming highly respected King's Counsels and William a Justice of the Supreme Court. Gowan, the renegade, chose medicine.

Emily's Uncle Thomas indirectly had a great influence on her life; from him she inherited a number of hatreds that, although wholly illogical, explained to her the psychology of family vendettas. Despite his "Fighting Tom" nickname, which seems to have been well earned (he was stoned once while electioneering as Member of Parliament for the family riding of Simcoe County, and had to have a bone removed from his skull), he was equally a peacemaker. At another time and another political meeting, when he appeared in danger of being trampled by the irate opposition, he drew down his cuffs, which had crept up a little, and said to his excited followers, "Quiet, my lambs!" Since then, Emily tells us, the County of Simcoe Conservatives have always been designated "the lambs."

With her "black hatreds" instilled in her heart by her uncle's political encounters, young Emily looked upon all opponents (of which her father and his brothers kept strict tally) as "dogs and infidels far beneath the dignity of human reproach." Years later she was shocked to learn that her mother had sold a piece of the family estate to one of the Tuckers: "A Tucker! Why—by God—it was a Tucker—this Tucker's grandfather—who once wrote an insulting verse about Thomas which became an election ditty, thereby earning the utmost mortification in the breasts of all our family."

On at least one occasion, the Ferguson Place welcomed some very celebrated guests indeed: Prime Minister Sir John A. Macdonald, Sir Charles Tupper and Mr. D'Alton McCarthy, who were attending an important political meeting in the neighborhood. That night Emily, who was given to reciting pieces of "a heroic and tempestuous nature" at the drop of a hat, gave a star performance reciting "Bernardo del Carpio" standing on a table in front of her illustrious audience. Sir John was also in attendance at her uncle's wedding. Among the other wedding guests was Mr. George L. Allan, the Governor of the Toronto jail, who had been pushed and held by a group of girls under a tiny hole in the marquee roof, through which rain was falling. Attracted by the squeals of the girls, Sir John approached and watched, with a serious face, the rain as it danced on the Governor's bald head.

"Well, Allan," remarked Sir John, "they have you where you've had many another good fellow."

"Where's that?" asked the Governor.

"Under the drop," replied Sir John, with a wink that conveyed infinite understanding.

The Fergusons certainly had the wherewithal to get the most out of life. Even the family crest indicated it. It was, in Emily's words, "A big Scotch thistle, from which a bee sucks honey—a bee with wings outspread.... It must have been a family characteristic the sucking of sweetness...from even a thistle."[3]

Isaac Ferguson insisted the children learn to write and speak properly, and arranged for a teacher in Barrie to come each Saturday to the village so that the children might learn the art of penmanship. "He would have none of those vain and inane flourishes that were taught in the public schools," says Emily. "No angular, cramped or backhand styles, and we must all write with a stub pen after the manner of the British folk. This is how, to this day, I can write for hours without so much as a twitch of a muscle much less a finger-ache." Her father knew, too, the pleasures of the classics, and when the Anglican Church of St. John's was built in Cookstown the children were packed off there to learn Latin. Emily went as far as *sui, sibbi, se,* before a change in plans sent her to school in the city.

Emily had little ability for music, and cut a sorry figure at the piano. Despite her parents' efforts to keep her at practice she only learned enough to render a few songs of a highly sentimental nature which her mother had learned from her mother and grandmother. It wasn't that she was unmusical, for she enjoyed the tunes her mother played so effortlessly, and the music of the village band that "soared into my brain like magic of a mighty wine." At such times Emily would feel capable of "the proudest achievements and even of physical braveries....For a certainty, there was never a band that could choke up the throat of a little girl like the one in our village."

In later years, a teacher of music asked her how it was that with long and flexible fingers and a quickness of sight, she was so timid in execution and so terrified of playing in public. "I was unable to give the reason, but maybe my first teacher—a man of misshapen spirit who was committed to the habit of correcting my fingers with his pencil—had something to do with my tremors.... It must be remembered too that when you sing or play, the audience can stare at you and still be polite."

She made this discovery when, at the age of ten, she sang in the Temperance Hall at a Sunday School concert. The song she chose for the occasion was "The Meeting of the Waters," a rather ambitious and most unsuitable selection for one of her tender years. When Christopher Cook, the rich and gallant bachelor of the village stood up and gazed directly at her, she forgot her song and subsided into the nearest chair, much to the mortification of her teacher, and, as she says, "Probably to the entire satisfaction of the audience."

It is not surprising that one to whom books became the staff of life should wonder later in life what books had impressed her most in her childhood. "Every woman," said Emily in "The Child I Used to Be" (published in a 1925 issue of *Western Home Monthly*):

should be able to tell the books that impressed her most during the formative years of her life, but I am unable to do so, unless the fact that certain books stand out more clearly than others. One of these was a volume entitled Foxe's "Book of Martyrs" from which I learned with horror of the power of life and death that is given into human hands. Also, in spite of my young intelligence, I learned that justice and judgment might be antithetical and that something was awfully wrong with the world. This must have been when I started my career as a reformer, but maybe it wasn't either, for even then I was filled with naughtiness and deliberately read books that had been forbidden by my father, a man of immense determination and one in no wise open to the influence of sugar.

Isaac Ferguson's strict views on what was fit reading for his children resulted, predictably, in wanton but surreptitious disobedience:

Novels were not fit reading for children and we were to be "scalped" if we read them. It was trying to have a near relative with such views, and it was not to be wondered at that I decided to read just the beginning and end of "The Children of the Abbey," "Ivanhoe" and "The Scottish Heroes" merely to see what novels were like.

It was a terrible fall though, for presently I was reading all about "Alkali Ike," "Three-fingered Bob" and other entrancing heroes whose remarkable adventures might be followed in a full seriatim known as "The Dime Novels." Of course there was risk in this. My father, sudden and sardonic, might descend upon the wood pile where we made our cave, and drag me forth to infamy. Still, there was my young brother, now a Supreme Court Judge, with high ideals for children, who used to stay on guard and warn me of the approach of the enemy with a soft, tentative whistle like a young blackbird trying its notes.... Then, it would be my turn to watch and whistle. Ah, well! They say in India—and the Lord grant it to be true—that sin without detection is sin dissolved.

But in every well-ordered home there is work to be done...

When not at games, or in mischief, we had work to do in the house or garden, which work was usually executed in "bees." Our special trials were polishing the knives and cleaning the lamps. Bath-brick was the clean-all of the day, and to secure desirable results the knives had to be rubbed on a board till they shone like morning sunlight. Still, one could scamp the knives upon occasion without serious risk of detection, but the lamp-glasses imperiously required cleaning. How I loathed those diurnal polishings and wick-trimmings! At our house it was in the lamp-glass the serpent lurked instead of in the wine glass.

In the holidays, before we were sent back to the city, we always drove to the third concession line and pulled a sack of green butternuts, which were placed in the attic to dry and brown against our home-coming in December. The thoughts of these, and of a barrel of brown sugar ready for immediate conversion into taffy, sustained me through the long, barren wastes of the Michaelmas and Christmas terms.

They were wondrous times, those flitter-winged holidays. Fruit and nuts at night were not leaden; tomatoes did not produce cancer, and sweets were not bad for the teeth. For the Easter holidays, my father, who was held locally to be a "good provider" laid in five gallons of maple molasses. Generally, we went with him to get it from a certain farmer whose name is of no consequence whatever, although it was George Duff. Such syrup as this Duff man made! seductive, amber stuff, the like of which I have never since tasted.

The family environment was one of affluence, accomplishment, affection and high ideals. Freedom of expression generally stayed within accepted bounds, the children being treated to a fairly benign form of discipline which allowed them their birthright of good-natured rebellion. Such rebellion might take the form of stealing apples from a neighbour's orchard, or, in the case of Tom and Gowan, smoking elm root in a rainproof room behind the woodpile while Emily stacked (and ate) the apples.

One of Emily's earliest recollections was of the coming of the railroad. She and her mother travelled on the long awaited "iron horse" to Collingwood to visit her Uncle Tom and her Aunt Fanny. They went to Guildford by stagecoach over a corduroy road that was "corduroyed exceedingly," and made her cry, then the narrow gauge to Collingwood, where Emily noticed the queer phenomenon that in the train the people sat still while outside it was the trees and houses that moved.

It was her first essay into the outside world and she felt shy and awkward, to the extent that on the evening of their arrival she stole away from the dinner table, hid in the drawing room and proceeded to give vent to a fair imitation of oaths and obscenities which habitually flowed from her uncle 'Miah when in distress.[4] This little exhibition failed to impress her cousin Isabella who pulled her from under the table, where she had fled, with the dire warning that if ever again she used such awful words God would strike her dead. "In looking back over my life," says Emily, "I can see that in backing up her assertion with a penalty, Isabella laid upon me a restraint that has proved almost unbearable, and which I had reason to regret in many similar social occurrences."

Chapter II

From Boarding School to Rector's Wife: 1883-1897

Forget always and absolutely that you are married—forget it, and laugh much; especially you must laugh.

In the 1880s Toronto was a city of about ninety thousand people, desperately coping with a continuous flood of immigrants, mostly from the United States and United Kingdom. Timothy Eaton (an Ulsterman) and Robert Simpson (a Scot) had opened department stores within hailing distance of one another, and small businesses were mushrooming all over town. Beggars were a common sight a few blocks from where the fashionable shopped and socialized; horse-drawn tram cars plied the streets, and wooden sidewalks were still in evidence.

At fifteen, Emily became a boarder at the Bishop Strachan School for Girls. Named after the city's first Anglican bishop, this prestigious private school had been a Toronto landmark for some fifteen years. Tom and Gowan were enrolled at Upper Canada College, a similarly elite school for boys of the wealthy and privileged, not far away.

It took a little while for Emily to get used to her new life, and for many months she was homesick, crying into her pillow each night, and marking off each day as it passed on a calendar. Gradually, however, she began to address herself thoughtfully to her studies, and became a praiseworthy student. Teaching at Bishop Strachan was by memorization and repetition, and the curriculum heavily emphasized the classics and religion. It might have been designed just for Emily. She excelled in both subjects, though, in typically restrained fashion, her report cards merely noted "Works admirably." She exchanged mudlarking for tennis, croquet and sedate walks with her botany class; she even began to enjoy music lessons. Emily discovered she had an encyclopedic mind (something her friend Nellie McClung would, in later years, remark upon with envy) and enjoyed reciting poetry to amuse herself and anyone else who would listen. Her great favorite was Robert Browning, and her volume of his poems is liberally underscored with notes of thoughtful interpretation. Every bare space in this book and others similarly cherished is filled with clippings and pictures carefully pasted into place.[1]

Emily at Bishop Strachan, aged 16

Emily made no close friends at boarding school, but her classmates liked her, and recognized her as a girl who was intensely earnest about her work, one with a definite aim, who set herself steadily and successfully to achieve it. Despite all this, she was at heart still the same fun-loving madcap who had enjoyed the daily rough and tumble companionship of her brothers at the one-room, red-frame schoolhouse in Cookstown...so that when Tom and Gowan presented themselves at the school one day to "take their sister out," she went, gaily, ready for anything that might transpire.

She found, awaiting her, a tall, blond, very good-looking young man with astonishingly blue eyes: Arthur Murphy.

Arthur was the eldest of the eight children of Frances and Andrew Murphy, Irish emigrants who farmed in Rosemont, sixteen miles from Cookstown. He was studying theology at Wycliffe College in Toronto. Although their paths had crossed before, since the Murphys and the Fergusons were—in those days—close neighbors, the gap in their ages (he was eleven years Emily's senior) had resulted in her total disregard of his existence up to now. Not so with Arthur, who had watched Emily grow from babyhood and obviously decided she would make an ideal minister's wife. He had taken the first opportunity, when they were all on "foreign soil," so to speak, to enlist the not unwilling aid of Tom and Gowan in arranging a meeting with her.

The school had strict rules against its young ladies consorting with members of the opposite sex whose relationship was not hallowed by consanguinity, so Tom and Gowan devised a plot to call on Emily at school; once beyond its confines, they handed her over to a waiting Arthur, a scheme that was repeated over the next few years.

Naturally, Emily was delighted at any opportunity for an hour or so of freedom. She was also quick to employ her not inconsiderable wiles for the provision of teas, goodies, boat trips and other treats on such occasions. Poor Arthur was undoubtedly called upon to pay handsomely for the course he had chosen. Given Emily's tender years, it was no love match at this stage but in later years it became so—a rich, warm relationship based upon mutual trust and esteem which supported them both in the dark days that were to come in their life together.

Emily looked forward to her meetings with Arthur. It was fun to be able to dress up instead of wearing the horrible school uniform. Her favorite was an ankle-length, high-necked dress, with a sash just below the waist in the fashion of the day. A wide-brimmed hat with an ostrich feather curled luxuriously around one side (almost over the left ear!) and shiny new high-button boots completed the outfit. She was a dark-haired young lady with a direct gaze and elfin features. Her small frame (barely two inches above five feet) showed no signs of the extra pounds it would carry in the years ahead when its owner persisted in her addiction to midnight snacks and all sweet things — particularly gooseberry tarts.

Dressing for one of these clandestine meetings, Emily found a mirror and regarded her reflection. How could she possibly not have noticed Arthur Murphy before? Admittedly he was old, all of twenty-six years, but how handsome he was! And, of course, older men were more interesting. The boys she met at home in the Christmas and summer holidays, friends of Tom and Gowan, with whom she would sometimes flirt outrageously, shocking the servants and meriting severe looks from Mama, were gangly youths compared to this latest "conquest." And what was that he had said on the first of their meetings? "Hurry and grow up so I can marry you." The nerve! But she rather liked it. It showed he had a sense of humor—even if he was going into the Ministry.

Pirouetting in front of the mirror she placed her feet in the third position for dancing, as she always did, and performed a sweeping bow. It would be years before she could marry, anyway, and who knew how many hearts she might break in the meantime?

Emily continued to flirt and fall in and out of love many times during the next four years. "But," as she said many years later, "there was never anyone, really, but Arthur." As for the object of these deliberations, he had already declared his intentions, and certainly he was not known to

Emily with her hair up for the first time

have seriously courted anyone else while he was waiting for Emily "to grow up."

Emily ultimately became Head of the Fifth and Sixth Forms and was the proud recipient of the Governor-General's Medal for Proficiency before she left school to become the bride of the Reverend Arthur Murphy.

On a summer's day in 1887, the little Anglican church of St. John's in Cookstown was to be the scene of the wedding of the year. The lively little brunette had finally come to realize that there never really would be anyone else but the very tall, very blond, very blue-eyed future minister of Christ; she had realized, too, that in his level-headed, commonsensical, unwavering approach to life, Arthur was the perfect mate for her. She could tease him unmercifully and rejoice in his good-humored tolerance which gave her high spirits full rein. At the same time, she had already come to know that this tolerance had its limits even for her, and to recognize the warning signs so that she could stop in time, change course—or take the consequences!

The weeks before the wedding passed in a whirlwind of activity. If the Fergusons and the Murphys were not throwing parties they were attending them; both families were well known in Simcoe County and had a wide circle of friends. The match received family as well as popular approval as both the bride's and the groom's mothers sailed into the social merriment with relish.

Arthur missed the revelries because, as a student priest, he had been inducted into the parish of Forest, a village some 160 miles southwest of Cookstown, not far from the shore of Lake Simcoe, and was busily establishing a home for his bride. Emily's weekly letters kept him informed of all the goings-on in Cookstown, however, so that he could share in some of the pre-nuptial excitement. He always remembered, even years later, the special fragrance that lingered about Emily's letters from the flower she always enclosed. This was the sort of thoughtful touch which typified all her dealings with people, whether they were loved ones or mere acquaintances. "When you talked to her," it was said of Emily in subsequent years, "she put everything else out of her mind."[2]

The wedding day, August 24, finally dawned. Attended by five bridesmaids in rainbow tints, Emily looked enchanting in white satin. The Murphy and Ferguson brothers made striking ushers, and the church was a veritable symphony of color, decorated lovingly by many village friends. A Toronto caterer sent waiters and food to the reception by train for the one hundred or so guests who had been invited to gather under the enormous marquee which had been erected on the croquet lawn.

If there were accounts of the Murphy's wedding in the newspapers of the time, they have not come down to us. Emily herself left no record of that day. She had not yet begun writing, but even after she had she was strangely uncommunicative about her wedding day. We can only conjecture that after the ceremony the newlyweds probably travelled to Barrie by road, stayed overnight and proceeded by train to Forest (via Georgetown) the next day. The train trip would have taken them a day, depositing them, with a cab the other end, late at night on August 25. A tiring journey for relatively few miles, but luxury compared to the boneshaking drive on the primitive roads.

Upon their arrival in Forest, Emily and Arthur proceeded to settle down in the little parish where Arthur had been so busily engaged the last few months.

Emily threw herself wholeheartedly into being a minister's wife. She took Bible classes, became president of the Missionary Society, played the organ, spoke at meetings, and organized entertainments and bazaars. She was, in her own words, "acquiring a stability that fitted me for later duties."

She was very young, however, and lacked as yet her husband's dedication and seriousness of purpose. There must have been times when she literally craved to be "one of the girls," to let her hair down, kick off her shoes and dance the Irish jig—and she loved to do just that. Right to the end of her life, even when her exalted position as magistrate precluded an abandoned fling around the ballroom, Emily's tiny feet could be seen tapping away under her skirts as she sat solemnly in civic dignity at one function or another.

It was her nature, when she rebelled at the formal dignity she was compelled to assume in her early married life, to kick over the traces and the consequences be damned. One day the new bride had playfully pelted a visiting group of clergy with apple blossoms from the orchard. Arthur had not been amused, but had suppressed his feelings at the time, and joined in the general laughter.

When they were alone, however, he had tackled the situation head on: "Em—I wish you would try and remember that you are no longer a schoolgirl but the resident clergyman's wife. Your conduct this afternoon was quite unforgivable."

"But Arthur, I was only..."

"You think only of yourself. It is quite time you grew up and..."

"That's not true! You're away so much and I get so...oh so...I don't know, lonely I guess. It seems..."

"I know, Cookie, (a pet name stemming from some past and futile attempt by Emily at cookie-making), but (he was weakening), please try and behave a little more in keeping with, uh, with..."

He couldn't go on, because now she was giggling. "What are you laughing at?" he demanded.

Emily pointed to the bed where Arthur's clerical robes had been neatly laid out by the new maid. "She thinks it's your nightshirt," she said, dissolving into peals of laughter.

Arthur looked—and a broad grin spread over his face.

The Sunday that Emily's laughter shattered the hush in church also shattered the serenity of her marriage. Pretension of any kind always amused her, and on this occasion something about the mincing step of the lady choir leader, as she made her way up the aisle, sent Emily off into peals of laughter. She tried to smother them—unsuccessfully; the whole congregation knew who was responsible for the interruption as Emily, the parson's wife, was seated in the front pew. "The Padre" (Emily's pet name for Arthur in all her books), "was terribly ashamed of me and I was so ashamed of myself that I went home [to Cookstown] for three whole weeks." But she bounded back, surprising Arthur shaving one morning. They clung together as though none of it had ever happened—and she got lather all over her face.

While Emily claimed that the incident marked "...one of my failures in my career as a parson's wife," the women of the parish put enough preserves and pickles in her cellar to last a year, and baked her a huge Easter cake as well as some puddings. They had also stitched her first baby's layette "from bandage to bonnet." "Who says," wrote Emily, "they hadn't forgiven me for betraying myself into a laugh that Sunday in church? And that they didn't like mothering the parson's wife, instead of having her mother them in the usually accepted style?"

Emily's laugh was to become something of a trademark in later years, after it had acquired, presumably, more timbre. William Arthur Deacon, a great friend, described it as "no ladylike titter, but something spontaneous and free and full throated."

For the next ten years the young couple were to go wherever the popular young clergyman was needed, but here in Forest, for three years, they began their life together. Within a year their eldest daughter Kathleen was born, but this happy event was overshadowed by the news that Emily's father, after months of suffering, had finally received his death warrant: cancer. Emily was griefstricken. She took the baby, at Arthur's insistence, and went home to be with her ailing father. But his agonies, her mother's frantic worries, and the general confusion of stunned family and friends, were such that she returned home with her grief.

Isaac Ferguson died the following year in 1889.

Shortly thereafter, Arthur received a ministerial offer from Watford, a few miles south. Only ten months into the posting the city of Chatham sent an urgent request for the young clergyman's services. Holy Trinity Church was twenty thousand dollars in debt and the congregation was dwindling. Would Arthur come and haul them out of their difficulties? By now, Arthur had achieved a considerable reputation as a man of accomplishment. His sermons were lively and graphic; he had boundless energy and a sense of dedication to his work; and he had another asset which had not gone unnoticed by the church hierarchy: a keen business acumen.

(About seven years earlier, a little girl who liked to dance and sing in public had come to Chatham with her father, who was hired as organist at Holy Trinity church. Her name was Leila Koerber and her specialty was Buttercup's song from *Pinafore*. Many years later she became famous as Marie Dressler, movie comedienne.)

The Murphys were to spend four years in Chatham, a town of twelve thousand about fifty miles from Watford. It was a city of mud and malaria when the Murphys arrived, and although they took quinine regularly, Emily was stricken. It took her months to recover.

In slavery days Chatham had been a refuge for escaped blacks from the American border; one part of the city was known as "Little Africa." "It is here," she wrote years later when she returned for a visit, "the negroes reside, and here you hie should you need a maidservant or a man to mow your lawn. These blacks are people of many virtues and some glaring defects. The negro cook has a dire genius for music, and her relations have fearsome appetites. She works hard, but, like grandfather's clock, stops short in a most irrational and wicked way. Still, it is highly unreasonable to expect a cook to observe all the commandments and eschew the seven deadly sins for a paltry five dollars a week."[3]

In an age not famous for its tolerance and understanding of minority groups, Emily was beginning to speak out. "Once they had a negro councillor here. He was black as Boanerges, but good and wise. Still, the white citizens were uncivil to him, and some showed an undisguised rancour. This used to trouble me, and I spoke of it to the late Master in Chancery. He was as gallant a gentleman as Galway ever produced, and I had the honourable satisfaction of his friendship. He agreed with me that this resentment arose from ignorance on the part of the whites. Precedent was against them.''[4]

Chatham market was a place Emily came to love dearly during the Murphy's tenure: ''I do not know,'' she wrote,

> any other market in Ontario where one sees more varied commodities for sale than at Chatham...I like the impetuosity of manner and graceful gesticulations of the French *femmes* who have homemade cheese, silver honey in the wax, garden herbs, and yellow squashes to sell. They have cream, and rabbits, and celery too, concerning which they babble to me in soft, sinuous vowels that are near to singing. Their manners are marked by *bonhomie*—that word for which, in English, we have no adequate expression. The women who have come to Canada from the southern states of America sell hominy, and cured tobacco that is tied in twists and bundles. Other women sell sauerkraut, russet apples, and sorghum, which is a thick brown syrup made from sweet corn...Turkeys are not sold by the pound on this market, but by their size. You may buy a bruiser for one dollar and fifty cents. And such geese, too! cleaned and skewered, and decorated with tiny sprigs of spruce, while, from their four quarters, giblets and livers peek out and fairly wink at the gourmand.[5]

It was in Chatham that the Murphy's second child, Evelyn, was born; she was as blond as Kathleen was dark, as perky as Kathleen was gentle and quiet. A third daughter, Madeleine, was born prematurely, due it is said, to Emily tripping over her nightgown and falling downstairs while she was carrying her. The child never grew strong, and a heartbroken Emily lost her in April, 1893, when she was just nine months old.

Madeleine was buried in the little church cemetery in Cookstown with a simple inscription on her grave: *Jesus called a little child unto Him.*

By 1894 Arthur had accomplished what he had set out to do in Chatham four years before. The church was debt free, and a fine pipe organ was installed. It was time to move on. When Ingersoll asked him to come and help in the renovation of St. James, he needed no further inducement; used as they were by now to moving from one place to another, the Murphys settled in very quickly.

Ingersoll was an old-fashioned little town named after an Empire Loyalist from Massachusetts, Major Thomas Ingersoll, in 1793.[6] It was here that the Murphys met James McIntyre, a local celebrity who became known

Arthur Murphy in 1894. "I fell in love many times in my teens, but there was never anyone, really, but Arthur"

as the Ingersoll Cheese Poet.[7] A furniture dealer and coffin maker in his more prosy moments, James McIntyre exploded into verse whenever he thought of cheese and cheesemaking; he was once "acclaimed" as "the worst poet Canada has produced—perhaps the worst poet in the English language."[8]

Undeterred, McIntyre read his poems at various public gatherings, and his fame quickly spread beyond the local borders. Ingersoll was, and still is, a prime cheese producing area, and in 1866, some thirty years before the Murphys settled there, local farmers put together a cheese that weighed three tons, and sent it to the New York State Fair. It was still intact three years later (and getting riper by the minute), when it was despatched to London for the 1869 Exposition. For a time prior to this, it had been exhibited in Toronto, and the event was more than enough to send McIntyre into poetic transports. He wrote an ode to the mammoth cheese, and a couple of stanzas were published in a magazine. A clipping is among Emily's papers...

We have seen thee, queen of cheese
Lying quietly at your ease
Gently fanned by evening breeze
Thy fair form no flies dare seize

Wer't thou suspended from Balloon
You'd cast a shade even at noon
Folks would think it was the moon
About to fall and crush them soon.

Sir John Willison, then editor of the *Globe* in Toronto, was so convulsed by McIntyre's poems that he started printing them in his paper. Eventually they were collected in two volumes, *Musings on the Banks of the Canadian Thames* (1884) and *Poems* (1889), which are almost priceless today.

The Murphys were living in an age of expansion which must have spread its excitement into the very bones of those who were fortunate enough to be a part of it. In 1893, during their stay in Chatham, the first Ford car had rolled off the assembly line; few people, including the Murphys, expected it to supplant the phaetons and the "g'langing of horses" [sic], a feature of life which, according to Arthur, would survive "till sun and moon have died."

Also by that time the second run had been made on the new intercontinental railroad, proving that it was, after all, no flash in the pan. And gold had been discovered in the Klondike at Bonanza Creek, Alaska, creating an unprecedented fever of excitement as prospectors rushed to procure the precious stuff. Not only were these major events happening on the world scene, but Canada was beginning to come alive with the birth of new ideas. It would take a few years, but Emily was to find herself a part of this new birth, urging it on, through her pen, her personality, her unbounded energy and zeal.

The advent in September, 1896, of Doris, a robust little girl, put new heart into Emily and she lavished all her pent-up affection on the baby. She was to be the last, and Emily might have sensed it. The selection of Doris's name effectively illustrates the encyclopedic nature of Emily's mind. In one of the Murphy scrapbooks she carefully noted on a card the etymology of the name and its classical associations.

With household help Emily had no difficulty finding time to involve herself in community affairs. She became embroiled in the controversy raging over the right of women to serve on church vestries, and wrote two letters to the *London Free Press* airing her views. "Of course women could contribute much to the administrative body of the church," she argued. One minister of the church reacted violently to this statement, saying he would resign if women were so privileged. Undaunted, the twenty-five-year-old Mrs. Murphy replied, sweetly, "Sir, you present us with a terrible alternative. I have no doubt, however, that we should become reconciled to your loss in time."

It was around this period that Emily tried to come to terms with her feelings about religion. From the unquestioning earnestness of childhood at her mother's knee, she had become unsettled in her faith, and at one point deeply involved in anti-theological thinking. It was, she said, undoubtedly the loneliest place on the curve of her religious life. She had lost the ability to pray. "How absurd it seemed," she wrote in retrospect,

> that I, the fly on the wall, should strive to guide the machinery! Indeed, I had gone further and believed with the old German mystic, Angelus Sibelius, that the will of God, by its very nature, was immune to petitions.
>
> To me, sin was no longer statutory—something to be penalized or wiped out by assent to a series of doctrines. Wicked people were only good material that was badly managed—a heterodoxy from which I have never entirely recovered. This period led me, for years, into a study of comparative religions, and of the Gods of Egypt with all their symbolism and strange enticement. I learned many things therefrom.

When she became a magistrate, Emily did her best to introduce "good management" and was surprisingly successful in many, if not all, her attempts to rehabilitate those upon whom she had to pass judgment.

Outwardly, Emily Murphy brought a devotion to her husband's principles and more orthodox beliefs, and was seldom absent from her front-row pew during his services. She particularly enjoyed the age-old chants of Evensong; the Anglican music would take her back again to the years of family churchgoing in Cookstown. But there must have been many times when she wanted to flee back to the family hearth and home where faith was comfortably explained and nourished. In later years she divided her religious life into four aspects:

> *The youthful and fervid*
> *The academic and doubting*
> *The maternal and social*
> *The older and peaceful*

Emily brought no blind, unthinking acceptance to her role as rector's wife, but a refreshing honesty which was characteristic of her entire approach to life. It was this integrity which endeared her to family and friends and confounded her enemies.

A cherished companionship began to unfold between husband and wife as Emily, tucked into the buggy or cutter beside her husband, accompanied Arthur on much of his parish visiting, she arguing, questioning, listening—

he explaining about his work, his hopes, his ambitions. During this time a camaraderie was born that provided a bedrock of mutual trust and respect upon which they would draw in the months and years ahead when conflicts of interest arose as the family grew up and needed Emily less, and she, flexing her own talents, took on the challenges which presented themselves.

In the long evenings when, daily visiting done, there were sermons to prepare and reports to be written, Emily put her creative talents to work, supplying just the right simile here, or colorful dramatic phrase there, filling immense leather-bound volumes with suitable stories and references for future use. She especially liked those which allowed full rein for invective and sonorous declamation. Arthur would wince now and again at an especially purple passage, and surreptitiously tone it down a little. But there is no doubt that Emily's encyclopedic mind and gift for words was a valuable asset to the young preacher, supplementing his own prodigious learning.

The three years the Murphys spent in Ingersoll were among the happiest in Emily's life. They had a lovely home, spacious and dignified, a large garden full of fruits and flowers. Warmth and gaiety flooded the house regularly as Emily played hostess with the same delight as her mother had done years before. Their tenure was marred only by the death in June of 1897 of William Robert Burke who had married Emily's sister Annie only a year before.

One evening Arthur came to Emily, troubled. The Bishop wanted him to leave his church work and become a missionary in Ontario. There was a vital need for men who could preach effectively to travel on missions about the province. There would be no set income, only whatever collections they might receive, no definite home, but a constant travelling through the hinterland of the province.

In recent years Upper Canada had undergone a historic church revival. Leaders of the ritualistic or "high" church of the Anglo-Catholics of Trinity College were locked in combat with the "low" or Evangelical Church of the Protestant Irish. A crisis, which had the Protestant Irish up in arms, resulted when a church manual was uncovered that proposed an extreme form of ritualistic teaching. The Church Association was founded to counter the new movement and preserve the more simplistic Protestant form of worship. Wycliffe College was eventually formed to train young men to go forth and preach the doctrine of the Evangelical Church. Arthur was one of these young men.

For Emily the change meant a complete readjustment of her physical and mental outlook. For two years life would be a succession of small hotels or the hospitality of mission members. Gone was the lovely house and garden, the income, the security and pleasure of being among friends. Now they were constantly on the move, strangers among strangers; after two weeks in one parish...on to the next. Emily saw very little of Arthur, immersed as he was in meetings, sermons, interviews and attendant details required of a missionary devoted to his calling—and there was always reading to be done. Arthur threw himself into his work with characteristic zest.

Although the Murphy income was now seriously curtailed, nursery help was cheap enough to ensure that the children were looked after wherever their travels took them. Time hung heavily on Emily's shoulders. She was bored. She began to nibble more than she should at her beloved sweet things. Gradually her small frame filled out to a matronly plumpness—not altogether unfashionable in a woman of thirty in those days, but a poor defence against the diabetes that years later — before the discovery of insulin — would ravage her body.

As the Missionary's wife, Emily was forced to take more interest in the problems of people outside her own circle of friends. She began to realize that there was a world far removed from the comfortable cocoon to which she was accustomed. In town after town she observed the terrible conditions under which the poor lived: crowded homes, no education, no jobs, too many children, and no prospects for a stable life.

Emily met and talked with the poor. At first they approached her hesitatingly, but her natural friendliness and aptitude for spontaneous questioning quickly put them at their ease. Her mind was sharpened by such encounters and she began to write daily, pouring out her interpretations of the poverty she saw on the backs of letters, envelopes, any piece of paper she could find. Written in diary form, her notes became her dominating interest, and later served as the basis for many of her published articles.

There was an unexpected change in Arthur's fortunes when he was invited to take his family and preach as a Missionary in England. In the excitement of making arrangements for this new adventure, Emily overcame her few misgivings at leaving family and friends. Arthur's enthusiasm and energy were infectious and she would never stand in the way of his advancement. She determined to look forward to the trip and enjoy every moment of it.

And so, on a July afternoon in 1898, the Cunard liner *S.S. Gallia,* steamed out of Montreal bound for Liverpool, with the Murphy family on board.

Chapter III

Impressions Of Janey Canuck Abroad: 1898-1900

We in Canada are always taking the attitude of second or third raters, are always borrowing our opinions from other countries instead of standing square and formulating our own.

"Going to sea," remarked Dr. Johnson, "is like going to prison with the chance of being drowned."

While this observation was made a hundred years before, passenger liners at the turn of the century left much to be desired. Charles Dickens, who made numerous crossings to give his successful readings in the United States, describes a storm at sea on the *Great Eastern* (probably during the winter months), that vividly illustrates the terror and havoc a great gale could inflict upon a ship plying the seas during the last years of the nineteenth century.[1]

Built in 1897, the *Gallia* was one of the Cunard's best ships. She had luxurious accommodation for three hundred first-class passengers in two-berth cabins, and room for 1,200 steerage passengers in 20-berth dormitories. She was steam-engined and barque-rigged, and her captain was under orders to use sail on every possible occasion. But in spite of her otherwise splendid first-class facilities, the *Gallia* had only two baths.[2] Passengers had to make their reservations for a bath with the cabin steward at a predetermined time, and then, as Emily described it, there was the quality of bathing to contend with. "If you are extremely anxious about it, and are not overly modest, you may have a hot salt bath in the morning, but otherwise when the angel prepares the water, like the man at the Pool of Bethesda, you will be pushed aside and another will step down before you."

For steerage passengers (there were only two classes at that time) conditions were, for the most part, appalling. Crammed into close quarters with rudimentary sanitation and poor food, disease and sickness were constant travelling companions, and deaths among steerage passengers were common.[3]

At six o'clock on the morning of July 5 the *Gallia* steamed down the St. Lawrence, reaching Quebec City in the early afternoon. "This gaunt, grey rock," noted an awestruck Emily, "is the centre milestone of Canadian history. Around its war-scarred heights, how many storms of history have

The S.S. Gallia *on which the Murphys travelled to England in 1898. It was on this journey that a challenge to her patriotism fired Emily into adopting for herself the pseudonym "Janey Canuck."*

broken!" That night she tried not to feel homesick as she saw Canada's shores retreating, and, clinging to Arthur, she half sobbed that she didn't want to leave. But, a few moments later, having pulled herself together, she snuggled into her "wooden overcoat" and slept.

Once out into the open sea Emily became seasick. "The steamer groans, sighs and grumbles in unison with me," she wrote. "I have nothing more to anticipate in this life...the limits of human endurance have been reached."

She recovered, however, discovered an appetite, and set out to enjoy herself. Meals on shipboard for first-class passengers were sumptuous. In the rivalry for supremacy on the lucrative North Atlantic run between the British and the Germans, in which the Americans soon joined, chefs employed by the steamship companies were expected to outdo themselves in the magnificence of their concoctions. In addition, British ships were still indulging in the special menus which they served to celebrate Queen Victoria's Diamond Jubilee the year before.

As others had before her, Emily found that on shipboard "the company falls into parties [and] natural selection is unconsciously established." Arthur quipped that this was "the old division of the bores and the bored," and managed to keep his distance from the group small talk, much to Emily's disgust: "...he has got an aggravating way of letting his chair back to the remotest angle, or of scowling at me as his natural enemy," she complained. "It doubtless secures him from troublesome intrusion and gives him time to be idle—very idle, or to think long, long thoughts about sermons and things."

Emily and Arthur explored the ship together; Emily likened the "stunning uproar and pulsing thuds" of the engine room to "a submarine inferno," but in typical fashion she talked to stokers, pretending to understand what they told her about the governors, pistons, cranks and valves. She also learned they worked around the clock — four hours on, eight hours off — for wages of twenty dollars a month.

It was on one of the *Gallia's* first evenings out that "Janey Canuck" was born. When a group of English people on board declared that, in their opinion, Canada was "a small community of fourth rate half-educated people, where local politics of the meanest kind engross the men, and petty gossip and household affairs the women," Emily bristled. "They spoke of our gruffness and bad manners," she said. "Perhaps it is so. I have not seen enough of the world to institute comparisons." But when one Englishman opined that Canadians "had the same nasal monotone and the tiresome habit of braggadocio" as the Americans, that did it. He was to feel the full effect of one Canadian's bluntness. "I told him," said Emily, "that Miss Isabella Baird, his countrywoman, had given as the result of many years' travel, the interesting decision that while the Americans were *nationally* assumptive, the English were *personally* so."

That night, Emily chose the name under which she would write from then on. "Johnny Canuck" was one nickname for a Canadian well known on both sides of the Atlantic; she would make "Janey Canuck" its feminine counterpart.

Soon they were off the coast of Ireland and crossing the Irish Sea, "the softest of the silken waters...and acutely green, like an ocean of melted emeralds." Then they were steaming up the Mersey and finally boarding the tender which was to take them ashore. Moments later the gangway slid out and the Murphys stood for the first time on English soil. The trip had taken ten days and fourteen hours.

On the cabman's advice the Murphys went to a large Temperance hotel where, much to Emily's delight, they had candles to light them to bed. Less delightful, however, was the way they were fleeced by mine host, "a rapacious Shylock," according to Emily, and they made a fast escape to new and cheaper lodgings where they lived *à l'Anglaise*: for two bedrooms, a sitting room and "attendance," they paid three guineas a week, purchasing their own food which the landlady cooked and served. That, and the cleaning of the rooms, was the "attendance." Coal, gas, laundry and so on were extras. They found it more expensive than Canada's equivalent, and Emily particularly was not amused at having to assume the responsibility of the family catering when she was travel-fatigued in a strange city. But there was no help for it, and so she sallied forth to forage for provisions.

"My shopping expeditions," she wrote, "were carried out in a state of bewilderment; not only because of the maddening currency, but by reason of the names of articles that hitherto I thought I knew. How was I to know that a 'pottle' was a peck, that 'corn starch' was corn flour, or that potatoes and apples were sold by the pound and that a layer cake was a 'jam sandwich.' Neither could I say whether I wanted a 'quartern' or 'half-quartern' loaf of bread, or whether I preferred malt or date vinegar." In due course she became used to the different ways and the family experimented with some of the national vegetables such as sea-kale, chicory, scarlet runners, endives and Brussels sprouts. They admired the long and delicious English cucumber and, on the whole, found English vegetables to be infinitely greater in variety and of better quality than Canadian, but more expensive.

While Arthur attended a large convention in Keswick, Emily had more time to look around and take note. She made the most of it, and was not entirely happy with what she saw. "Everywhere," she said, "I noticed flashily dressed women who are avowedly and unblushingly disreputable." She condemned their "sidelong glints and encouraging smirks to all male-comers" as "allurements to sin." She had no premonition how closely she would, in later years, become connected with this unfortunate human flotsam when she said, "this life with its vile wage must be a great temptation to kitchen drudges, who see only the fine clothes and not the sad *finale.*"

Emily was observing a side of life in a great seaport far removed from that which she had known in Cookstown, Chatham and other even smaller Ontario towns. Begging and abject poverty were rampant, and Emily was obviously shocked and dismayed by the "poverty-distorted children" and the vulgar language they used. She was also severely critical of the "bareheaded drabs, clad only in shawls and draggled skirts," who "reeled foul-mouthed and beer be-sodden from the low groggeries." Emily had even more of a tongue-lashing for the men, who looked "positively oozy, and reminded you of a beer-soaked sponge that you have only to touch to make the fluid come out."

Despite her scathing words, Emily was obviously moved deeply by the terrible conditions which surrounded her. It is likely that her experiences in Liverpool, combined with her natural compassion and the extra years of maturity which time would bestow, stood her in good stead many years later when, as a magistrate, she was charged with the task of dealing with various "allurements to sin" and the results thereof.

On a more positive note, Emily was struck with the massive city buildings, "built for eternity," though she could not abide the smoke and "grimy incense of half a million chimneys." She loved riding the omnibuses, and with the children went sightseeing on them at every opportunity. The horses, she noted with satisfaction, mostly came from Canada. "Staid, magnificent, sober minded, incapable of surprises, with their glossy hides and well padded contours, they are a credit to our young colony."

Before the Murphys left Liverpool one rainy day in August, Emily combed the docks via the overhead railway, her mind boggling at the sight of shipping extending for nine miles in length. Her further peregrinations took her to St. James cemetery where she saw the unusual tombstones noted by Nathaniel Hawthorne when he visited it in 1853, in particular one of Sara Biffin, a celebrated miniaturist who, born without hands or arms, painted with her mouth. Emily was just in time, for shortly thereafter the cemetery was filled in with clay.

Visits to various churches to compare ceremonies gave Emily much room for thought. Impressed by the sermons delivered to packed congregations, she made notes for Arthur. Her stoutly Protestant mind found the ceremonies performed by the Ritualistic Church "highly theatric, and, without the clouds of incense, had been [sic] entirely trivial and vulgar." "This church," she reported, "was showered by stones on the next Sunday, by the Evangelical pugilists of the Church Militant, and the clergy roughly handled, for it would appear that the dogs of war are loose, and the end is not yet." Emily's pacifist heart deplored such tactics. It was the constant infighting between the two religions (which she had grown up with amidst the bitter wrangling of her Irish Protestant and Catholic kin) which led her to question the validity of either denomination.

Emily was admittedly bewildered by the perplexities of the Church reform crisis and Home Rule for Ireland. Embroiled in dispute, the protagonists had forsworn inspiration for theological bickering. "Most earnestly do I wish to see the establishment reformed," she wrote, "for the sake of its greater security and its greater perfection, but whether reformed or not, may God in His mercy save us from the calamity of seeing her destroyed."

In August, the Murphys left Liverpool by a train which plunged them into tunnel after depressing tunnel before reaching London. "It is good advice," said Emily, with a caustic wit for which she was to become famous, "never to go under ground until you are put there."

England unfolded before them—from the glory of her countryside where "the fields appear to be perfected by a hairdresser rather than a ploughman," to "the congested brick and mortar...grime and sordidness" of the London they passed through on the way to the gaily colored throngs of Southend.

Emily's roving, ingenuous eye and her endlessly enquiring mind missed very little. She could be acidly critical of her host country in one breath and rush to its defence the next second. Anarchy, socialism, Christianity and capitalism were all subject to her exacting pen—as were society's blunders. On the steamer which the Murphys took to Clacton one night was a girl with "phossy jaw," a common term for necrosis or matchmakers' leprosy, caused by inhaling the fumes of the phosphorus used in tipping matches. "First signs of the disease," wrote Emily, "are when the teeth ache and then drop out. Later the loathsome leprosy eats its way into the roof of the mouth and inside the nose, when the jaw drops off." This and probable blindness too, for a pitiful $1.92 per week, before a merciful death would overtake the victim. "Who is responsible?" fretted Emily. Typically, she was the only traveller on the boat who spoke to the tragic girl.

One can sense Emily's mental groping at this time in her life as her natural compassion for the downtrodden, and innate hatred of injustice vied with a repugnance that came out of her genteel, class-conscious upbringing.

In Southend the Murphys discovered English teas before proceeding to Shoeburyness where Arthur was to speak at an artillery station. The guns did not interest Emily, but she enjoyed her tour around the married quarters, which on the whole met with her approval. A rectory picnic and pheasant shooting at a weekend house party at Westcliff rounded out the Murphys' schedule before they headed back to London in October.

On the subject of shooting, and in fact all blood sports, Emily was unequivocal: she did not sympathize. She noted that the game was "so plentiful that I cannot see how the shooting of it can be called sport, for there is absolutely no precariousness about it." Arthur, on the other hand, loved all game sports; it was a subject, like many others, they had to agree to disagree on in order to keep the peace between them.

In London they took the children to the zoo and had a hard time enticing them from the monkey house, where they were transfixed by a lemur who was dying of consumption. He had a wracking cough, uncanny staring eyes, and a voice like a banshee. Best of all were the elephant rides on Jingo, which Emily likened to "a storm at sea"; she was thankful when she descended from his "bony and twisted irregularities" and found herself still alive.

One of the highlights of Emily's stay in London was the day of the Lord Mayor's Show. She was determined to see it, but despaired of finding a vantage point amidst the spectators, all of whom seemed to be bigger and taller than she. Then she noticed some urchins perched on the stone balustrades of St. Paul's, and persuaded two of them to give up their places by flashing a shilling at them. It was a high climb, "but presenting a bent knee to them, they lifted me as though to mount a horse." Even some rude remarks from bystanders about an unwarranted display of ankles and garters failed to dim Emily's joy at having got a seat worth several times what she paid for it, and the opportunity to shout and clap her hands when the procession went by.

On December 23 the two older Murphy children were boarded at a private school in St. Albans, Hertfordshire, just outside London, an interesting old Roman city to which Emily returned often to see the children and to take them exploring.

Emily was now free to take bus rides around London, trying to recall her English history as she came across the house of a well-known bard or historical figure.

After a visit to Smithfield she drew morbid comparisons between the religious warfare then being waged between the Protestant and Roman Catholic Churches and the fanaticism of the fourteenth-century witch burnings carried out at what became known as Ruffian's Hall, Smithfield:

> Here, the flames licked up the life of the beautiful Anne Askew, she having been brought hither in a chair, because forsooth, my Lord Chancellor Wriothesley, "stockish, hard and full of rage" had almost torn her body asunder on the rack, and so she was unable to stand on her poor dislocated feet. To this spot too, came John Bradford, John Rogers, and a host of other "Holy men who died here martyred and hereafter glorified." It was a hard problem the church had to solve, for what could she do with men who passed to their death with light steps, and the words on their lips, "This is life eternal." Their bones, with scarce a semblance of humanity, were buried where they fell, and now a tablet marks the spot.
>
> To the memory of these saints, and that of my own good ancestors, who suffered and died for the sake of the Protestant religion, and the liberties of England, I laid a wreath of laurels on the stone, all the while repeating mentally some lines, the burden of which was "Lest we Forget."

The Temple Bar memorial on Fleet Street incurred Emily's displeasure. "It is the most hideous thing I have seen in England," she exclaimed. "Why the effigy of a beast, half eagle and half lion, should perpetuate the fame of Temple Bar is not clear, and one tries to find justification for what appears to be a very bad joke."[4]

During a visit to the Inns of Court, Emily learned that a lawyer is not permitted to speak unless he is bewigged and gowned. If the judge asks for him he says: "I am present your Lordship, *but I am not visible."* "I was glad to know this," says Emily, tongue in cheek and with no foreknowledge of her own future connection in this field,

> for it gives me ever hereafter the legal authority of the first Court in the world to state that I am not visible to callers if not properly coifed and robed.... A lawyer who once had to speak for sixteen hours, obtained permission to lay aside his wig, but with the stipulation that this permission was not to be made into a precedent. I can understand now why justice is not more often done. The wig, not infrequently, covers both ears of the judge and so prevents his hearing either side of the case.

When asked by someone (nicknamed "The Ancient" by Emily) whether he would like to become a lawyer, Arthur's reply was succinct: "It is easier to preach than to practice."

It is evident that Emily was strongly affected by the poverty and degradation she saw in places like Whitechapel in London's East End: "One cannot fail to observe the numbers of women with bruised faces—women who appear to have drained the draughts of poverty to their very lees. They are having their hell in this world, no matter what may lie in store for them in the future." When similar conditions confronted her in Canada many years later, producing victim after victim for sentencing, there can be no doubt that her introduction to the seamier side of life in this teeming city shaped her thoughts and enabled her to bring a much needed positive and humane approach to the handling of each problem.

There were weekly visits to the City Temple to hear "the trenchant utterances" of a Dr. Joseph Parker, and one evening they both joined an international Protestant rally at the Royal Albert Hall with ten thousand others, including six hundred clergymen. Days later, an address at St. Bride's by the Archbishop of Canterbury was declared dull by Emily. "Indeed," she said, "I have a shrewd suspicion that a Canadian parish in the back countries would probably starve him out." However, the Archbishop did have the ability to keep his address short, which gained him some favor.

Emily's first ride in a horseless carriage ("on the whole I prefer the horses") was to Chelsea where she visited Thomas Carlyle's house. "I touched the copies of Carlyle's works as sacred things, and why not? His writings were no mere empty masks. You can feel his heartbeats in them." All of Emily's adulation was reserved for the "sage of Chelsea;" there was none for his wife, Jane Welsh Carlyle, "whose carpings were often the result of tingling nerves and 'low spirits'..." Emily was perhaps unaware that the Carlyle house had no running water, and while the great man had sat in the attic wrestling with his histories, his wife had toiled down below with the servant producing hot bath water and banishing dirt. Under the circumstances, Mrs. Carlyle might be forgiven a few "low spirits."[5]

Visits to the Royal Mint and "the gruesome gehenna" of Newgate prison were fitted in before a quick trip to Plymouth and the West Country. Tea at the Vicarage in St. Budeaux produced an observation from Emily on the subject of class distinction. "These English," she said, "have no jealousy of social disparity. On the contrary, they are proud of "the quality." The lower classes," she went on, "confine themselves to their caste and do not aim at imitating the manners of their betters, but when these same classes come to Canada, they at once affect an officious air and familiarity that are most objectionable."

In Devon the Murphys spent a day "out to doors" (local parlance) at the seat of the Earl of Mount Edgecumbe, munching on a host of good things including "clouted" [sic] cream. Following on the heels of this agreeable day was a visit with the local curate to the human shambles of the slum district where "we warily groped our way up dark staircases by the aid of ropes, through mouldering garbage and trodden-down nastiness." Learning that the municipality had forced the landlords to place these ropes to prevent the unfortunate tenants from taking headlong plunges in the dark, Emily wrote: "It began to dawn on me what 'knowing the ropes' meant." It also dawned upon her how little influence the Church had upon "the lapsed masses." "They are blankly indifferent," she wrote, "and faith is sick—very sick."

In Westminster Abbey, next on the agenda, Emily pronounced The Nightingale Monument to be the finest in the Abbey. This memorial appears to have stirred a variety of emotions, including those of Oliver Goldsmith ("remarkable") and John Wesley ("affecting"). Emily was a little more expansive: "The iron doors of the grave have been burst open by the skeleton figure of Death. He is aiming his pitiless arrow at the lady, whose agonized husband vainly endeavours to shield her from the enemy. It is a frenzy of love in stone."[6]

Everything, even the aggravating policeman who kept her moving past the frescoes in the Houses of Parliament, was forgotten the day Emily actually had a close and unobstructed view of Queen Victoria on her way from the Palace to lay the foundation stone of the Victoria and Albert Museum in South Kensington. Emily and Arthur had taken up their stand at Hyde Park Corner. In painstaking detail Emily describes the crowds, the good-natured policemen, the procession of guards, footmen, nobility and royalty, and finally—the Queen's coach: "Her Majesty sat in one corner and looked small—even tiny. She wore a dowdy looking gown and a black bonnet, adorned with a white feather...I do not know whether the crowd cheered or not. I could not hear. I was so intently watching the dear, faded little mother, who has stamped her name and character on the world's golden age. God bless her! As queen of our hearts, she reigneth alone!"

That evening, for a change of pace, the Murphys attended the annual meeting of the Women's Temperance Association. Emily at this time was very much an advocate of Temperance, a stand she subsequently reversed years later when she realized that alcoholism could not be abolished in such a simple fashion.

The Murphys had been in England for almost a year when Arthur was invited to preach in Homburg, West Germany.[7] Suffering from an attack of sciatica, Emily remained in England until her husband, convinced that the mineral baths and waters of the famous German spa would be beneficial to her, returned suddenly to the U.K. to take her back with him. He obviously caught her by surprise for, she says, "I had only eight hours to gather in my laundry, my new frock (half completed) and take a hurried run to St. Albans to see the bairnies."

Emily's first impression of Holland was made from across a heaving Channel: "...it needs to be strained or wrung dry. It is half submerged. It is amphibious. The people live on the sink or swim principle.... Surely

Emily Murphy in England, where she first became acquainted with the grinding poverty and corruption she would later face as a magistrate

Holland is the peasant's heaven. The ground is so rich that '...tickle [it] with a hoe, and it laughs with a harvest!'"

She found Rotterdam "dirty, unkempt and featureless" and Germany, by contrast, "a land of vineyards and olive yards and of brooks that run among the hills." Down the Rhine en route to Koln, Emily was overcome by the July heat and was too ill to even crane her neck out of the window. Sympathetic fellow travellers drenched her with eau-de-cologne, which provided some relief.

They arrived at Homburg "the lovely Tanus town," late in the evening and were rather overwhelmed by the welcome given them by their landlady with whom Arthur had been staying. Warm baths, tea and bed were joyfully arranged, and three-year-old Doris, who was accompanying them, was patted and petted and made much of by Frau Becker and her maids. As Kathleen and Evelyn are not mentioned in *Impressions of Janey Canuck Abroad* during this period, one assumes they were left behind at school, a fate which often befell the children of English parents.

Life amidst the worldliest society in Europe was a considerable culture shock for the Murphys. Emily does not seem to have been overly impressed by the efficacy of "the waters," stoutly maintaining that "the early rising, the walk before breakfast, a plain diet and life by schedule," were probably necessary adjuncts to any curative process. The Kaiser Wilhelm bath-house was something else again. An imposing building housing eighty-four rooms, it was a mecca for "victims of spleen, obesity, gout, rheumatism and anaemia both mental and physical.... In it, you sweat and frizzle in baths of mud, pine, electricity and vapour. If your purse and constitution will stand it, you may take inhalations galore, or the water, gymnastic and massage cures." Outside the baths, a Swiss prepared and served goats' milk whey. "We drink deeply," she said, "and try to believe it most beneficial."

The Kurhaus gardens with their "ravishing music" enthralled them both, but Emily cautioned against a woman strolling there unaccompanied, lest she be opportuned by "loose moralled Englishmen with evil and unmentionable purpose." The stately Kurhaus, once a gambling casino but now given up to more innocent pursuits, was the scene every summer evening of a dress parade on its piazza of the beautiful people of the day. "Up and down they go," wrote Emily, "Russian princesses with costumes fearfully and wonderfully made, the wives and daughters of Ambassadors, English duchesses alarmingly *décolletée,* beautiful Americans, and wealthy Jewesses. Down the long walk, too, lounges Adelina Patti and her boy-husband. Her hair is dyed the new shade. Known as 'Tuscan red.' Her jewels would buy a small kingdom."

How she drank all this in, the young woman from small-town Ontario!

Gretchen now entered their lives. Engaged to look after Doris, she was "the most sullen savage in Germany," a probably unmerited description due more, I suspect, to Emily's limited knowledge of German than to the girl's own nature. "My attempts at making her understand what I require of her are as ludicrous as they are useless," Emily grumbled. "One day I told her I was not well, and sent her to bring over my dinner from a restaurant. An hour later, the girl reappeared looking particularly happy. She had gone to the restaurant and had eaten my portion."

Arthur was offered the Church in Homburg but declined it; the five month season would have meant seven months of enforced idleness "and that," noted Emily, "would be sheer torture to one of such an active temperament. Besides," she added, "he likes roving better."

The church services were well attended in Homburg, some coming for the prayers, others for the sermon and yet a third group for the Communion. The Royal Pew, reserved for the Prince of Wales, a frequent visitor to the Spa, was usually occupied ("when the Padre prays for the Royal family, he can look down and see them there. He must also include in the State Prayers...the names of the German Imperial Family and the President of the United States"). What impressed Emily, who could be awestruck in the presence of the exalted, was to Arthur all in a day's work. "The Padre preaches to all these grandees as if they were very simple people and regulation every-day-sinners given to gambling, lying, sensuality and hypocrisy, which is most likely."

Even Arthur was surprised one day, however, to discover that the little boy whose head he had been patting while talking to his mother was destined to become the King of Greece.

The Padre

Before leaving Germany the Murphys paid visits to the Emperor Wilhelm's summer palace at Homburg (the Emperor was absent at the time), the international tennis tournaments, and the Tanus Mountains to rest, read and sleep. Emily enjoyed these "bird flights to the black forests" where they would sometimes buy rusks at the Swiss Chalet, dipping them in the Rhenish wine called Dragon's Blood and pretending to be Canadian red squirrels eating beech nuts.[8]

On the subject of German food Emily was noncommittal, though she admitted to having gained quite new ideas of the possibilities of veal, and being quite moved by the distinctively German baked apples, with lemon peel, sugar and brown meat gravy. Noting that the *Weinkarte* was much in evidence on every table, and that the customer was charged extra for dinner if wine was not ordered, Emily wondered about the adverse influence upon German society of such loose standards. And yet during their stay they did not see a single case of intoxication, leading her to conclude, "There does not seem to be any room here for the W.C.T.U. [Women's Christian Temperance Union]."

An invitation to the Murphys to join "The Lords of the Council and all the nobility" at their luncheons and many tea drinkings, surprised and delighted Emily, who took advantage of the opportunity to study at close quarters the details of dress of the great ladies of fashion and their refined manners. It was something of a disappointment. When they began to criticize the American socialites, who figured prominently on the European scene at the time, for "overdressing, twanging and posting," Emily, who was inclined to think their harsh words were caused more by jealousy than anything else, promptly jumped in, characterizing the American girls as "clearwitted, vivacious and brilliant conversationalists, and quick to assimilate new ideas." To further drive home her point, she said it was no wonder the American girls were walking off with all the eligible Englishmen in sight.

Back in London, completely cured of her sciatica, Emily was once again sightseeing. A quick trip to Wolverhampton, to stay in a beautiful old Rectory "swathed in roses," quite captivated her. She got into a discussion one day with the rector on the relative merits of English and Canadian plums, and was moved to recount the story of Arthur and the Bishop of Huron. The Padre had taken the Bishop to visit a prize farm at Chatham... While waiting for the farmer to appear, the Bishop helped himself to some choice plums which lay in great heaps on the ground. On the arrival of the host, the Bishop made profuse apologies, saying "I fear, my dear sir, we are making too free with your plums," to which the farmer replied that he was quite welcome as they were for the pigs anyway.

"I shall not write about the beauties of the Crystal Palace," said Emily, "because I did not see them. It is a huge, ugly pile, great only by size. The building was pathetically expensive, and its chief value is in demonstrating how easy it is to spend seven million dollars." However, she did write of the many things she did see—a hotly contested game of polo, the picture galleries, museum and various splendid exhibits all housed under the enormous glass roof, plus an enthralling ascent in a captive balloon to an altitude of one thousand feet. She missed the last bus home due to a magnificent firework display, and so arrived back footsore and weary, but happy.

Of course she "did" the Art, Science and Natural History Museums of South Kensington, bewailing the "slapdash style" of her visit. The National Gallery was the scene of a spirited argument between Emily and her mate on the subject of Dutch painting, which Emily thought "ugly in its extreme realism." This led Arthur to accuse her of being "ignorant of the first principles of art," and the conversation went downhill from there.

In November, 1899, Emily visited the army barracks in Colchester, where Arthur had spent the previous two weeks speaking to the soldiers. She reported that when orders came for the men to be ready for immediate transportation to South Africa, the army hospital was full of sick privates.

"In three hours there was not a solitary man in bed." The Boer War was on, and "every mother's son...was ready to lay his body down to fertilize the soil of an African veldt."

A few days later, the Murphys watched the departure of the soldiers from Waterloo station to the accompaniment of tearful families and "the throbbing of the drums." "There were many tear stained faces," wrote Emily, "and hearts that ached, too, for these tough-fibred sons of Mars, led out like sheep to the slaughter, for it will be a mere handful who come home again."

A pacifist all her life, she was to write bitterly about the impending conflagration of 1914-18, but when it happened, she worked furiously to harness the war effort at home. In the late twenties, she saw, long before most did, that Europe was heading once more into a black pit of human suffering, and she campaigned in print and on the podium to warn against it. She died before her worst fears were realized.

On the strength of her long tenure in England, Emily developed some dogmatic opinions regarding the social life and traits of the inhabitants. She characterized the Englishwoman as

> either a lady or not a lady. Perhaps this is the only way in which as a sex they are particularly emphasized. Lacking in individuality, solid but not brilliant, wanting in tone but not insipid. An English lady has a high sense of her moral obligations...If rich she keeps a small army of servants, and if poor, does not make the work of living too hard, but reduces her housekeeping to a very simple system.

As to the Englishwoman's husband,

> ...his chief characteristic is pride...he does not like foreigners, and above all the inhabitants of America. He does not think much of the prospects or wealth of a nation that is expressed as a decimal system instead of in pounds...If you are a Canadian he is mildly surprised at the fairness of your skin. He had an idea you were half French and half Indian. It must be that the hot-air furnaces in the colonies bleach your complexion. He is distinctly charmed when he finds you do not eat with a knife. As he does not of necessity read the daily papers, he sneers at your passion for news, and dubs you 'the inquisitive Canadian.' To summarize him brutally, he is a queer conglomerate of obstinacy, pride, justice, refinement, acquisitiveness, hard-headedness, bravery and sensuality.

On November 7, 1899, the Murphys were on their way home from Liverpool. We have to forgive Emily her lack of charity when she spoke of the 350 "filthiest sweepings of the Old World" who swarmed aboard the ship as steerage passengers. It was a time when the haves were inclined to walk away from the smell of the have-nots. To Emily's credit, she was among the first of her generation to realize that walking away from poverty and unsavory conditions was no solution to it, and she did much in later years to make amends. "Right now," she said, "every one of them is looking out grandly into the future [in the better land of Canada] with unbounded faith."

For six awful days they were subjected to the worst battering that God and Mother Nature could devise. "They go down alive into Hades," wrote Emily as the boat shook like a huge, writhing monster.

> As the vessel leaped and swung, there was a crashing accompaniment of broken plates and bottles and a queer hurly-burly of cutlery. Thud after thud came the huge rollers, with mad impetuosity on the deck, an occasional wave finding its way down the halls and into our staterooms. Yet it was grandly awful, this dread shrieking and the wild clangor and moan of the storm, and as one listened through the long watches of the night, now and then you prayed for the lonely man lashed to the bridge.

Emily had less benevolent feelings, however, toward the occupant of the next cabin:

> The boat was turned to face the storm and for two days we travelled out of our course. On the ninth day the ship stopped dead. The screw had been out of the water so frequently that the packing had worn out and in its present condition we were making only three knots an hour. I was staggering along the corridor when the extremely cross old woman in the next stateroom put her head out of the door. She looked frightened. Why had the boat stopped? At that moment, my innate germ of original sin asserted itself, and in a low tone that could mean anything appalling, I told her that the boiler might burst any second, and then, by dint of marvellous balancing, hurried on.

Arthur was chaplain for the voyage and in his official capacity they visited the steerage quarters. The stench drove them back at first. Braving "the soul sickening reek" they were horrified to see the women (men were in separate quarters at the other end of the ship) lying around in their own filth, many of them ill, others half naked. Emily notes that horses were often carried in this part of the vessel and "There is no nonsense here about modern sanitation." Disgusted and shocked, they left with words of sympathy to some English women—'We could not talk to many for it was a strife of tongues'—and a gift of oranges and apples, which Emily had taken with her.

It was to be another decade or so before steerage accommodation was abolished as such, and improved third class facilities took its place.

"It was good to see Newfoundland in the distance," wrote Emily, "its shore hugged by a pearl grey mist, for it was Canada, and we were gliding gently to the haven where we would be. The Padre told us that in the privy purse of Henry VIII there is this curious entry: 'To the man that found the new isle, ten pounds.' This man was Cabot, the island lay before us."

To say that Emily was glad to be home would be putting it mildly. She was in raptures! "We got up at five o'clock to see the Laurentians; it was the most beautiful sight that had ravished our eyes since we left home. 'Dress'd in earliest light,' the mountain tops blazed in the sky like altars of beaten gold. They seemed a mirage of the god-lit hills of heaven.

"We spent the last and fourteenth night aboard ship, on the St. Lawrence. The steamer's talons were dropped on the river bed and we lay at anchor, once more in the first, best country, God's fairest gift to man—the land of the Maple."

Chapter IV

Dangerous Places: 1900-1903

The only truly contented women are those who have both a home and a profession.

During the couple's absence abroad, Emily's mother had moved to Toronto to be closer to "her boys." Tom, William and Harcourt had all graduated in law, and were practising at the Ontario Bar. Sister Annie had also moved to Toronto since the untimely death of her husband, William Burke, shortly after their marriage.

It was a wild and joyous affair when the family assembled at their mother's house on Emily's and Arthur's return.[1] Missing was Gowan, who had gone into medicine and moved to Great Falls, Montanta, after studying in Europe. This had been a disappointment to Mrs. Ferguson, who firmly believed that a family's place was together. Nor had she been in favor of Emily and Arthur gallivanting off to Europe, and lost no time upon their return in letting them know that she hoped they had got such nonsense out of their heads. She adored the children, particularly chubby little flaxen-haired Doris, and loved nothing better than to see all her family gathered about her table.

Mrs. Ferguson still liked to dress meticulously—beautifully tailored black silk dresses were her favorites—and she relished the compliments the boys good-naturedly paid her. Emily recalls one time when her mother came into the sitting room looking very elegant in a new dress, and flushed with pleasure when Will whispered loudly, "Some class to the cows in our pasture!"

Arthur was welcomed, with Emily, back into the bosom of his thriving family. His diminutive mother clasped her son in her arms as though she would never let him go. Two of her other sons, William and Robert John, had also become ministers, and James had taken up farming in his father's footsteps. Richard, her fifth boy, was training for the Army at the Royal Military College in Kingston; the three girls, Elizabeth, Phoebe and Mary, were all happily married.

Arthur's father, almost as tall as Arthur, shook his son's hand with a firm grip. He was a gentle man of few words, but they both knew that nothing needed to be said on this occasion. The warmth of the brightly burning fire and the gaiety of the young people flooding the house was sufficient.

The Ferguson family. Seated l-r: Thomas Roberts,
Mrs. Ferguson, William. Standing l-r: Annie,
Harcourt and Emily

Christmas came and went, and a new century arrived. Arthur was still on the staff of the Church Parochial Mission Society in England, at a comfortable salary, and continued his mission work in Canada. This entailed journeys to the Maritimes and the Western provinces. Sometimes Emily accompanied him, but mostly she remained in Toronto in their home near High Park.

Kathleen and Evelyn were enrolled at Havergal College, while Doris ("Little Girl Blue" as her mother called her) stayed at home. Emily was devoted to her youngest daughter and the two of them shared happy times together feeding the squirrels and pigeons in the park, Emily watching anxiously as the little girl clambered merrily, and sometimes unsteadily, up and down too many trees. They visited the toylands in the downtown department stores, stopping on the way for some candy, and later returning home by horsedrawn cab or bus. It was an enchanted time for the two of them, and Emily poured all her pent-up devotion into amusing her little daughter. She arranged to continue the dancing lessons, too, begun in the Golden Hall at Homburg where Doris had learned her first steps in magnificent surroundings among classes of Italian, French, English and Spanish children.

Around this time Emily was busy preparing her manuscript for publication. Arthur had already published a volume of his sermons under the title *The Way of Life,* which was soon to go into its second printing, and she was keen to see her own work in print too.

On January 22, 1901, Queen Victoria died in her 82nd year, marking the end of an epoch. Her son, Edward, succeeded her and launched Britain into an era of almost unparalleled, and certainly much needed, gaiety. In her waning years of sorrowing widowhood, the old Queen had wrapped a blanket of lugubriousness around the British nation which it threw off with relief when the fun-loving Prince of Wales was crowned Edward VII. Much of this relief spread to the colonies, and in Canada a spirit of adventure was in the air, which augured well for new pursuits in almost any endeavour, particularly literature and the arts.

Dedicated "To my fellow traveller, The Padre," *The Impressions of Janey Canuck Abroad* was published in 1901. A slim volume of 186 pages, poorly proofread, it was anything but handsome and must have disappointed Emily considerably. Although it contained (according to its preface) "Little in the semblance of novelty for the well-informed traveller," it offered, as we have seen, a different insight, at times a sparkling wit, and an honest, if sometimes ingenuous, appraisal of a multitude of things. *Impressions* successfully captured the depth of Emily's general knowledge as well as her natural talent for rigorous analysis. Its immediate success in England guaranteed its success in Canada. The name of Janey Canuck began to become known, not only to literary circles, but to the general public.

One day, Emily and Arthur were dining at a private club run by Joseph Phillips Esq., president of the York County Loan Company, and future president of the Toronto Life Insurance Company. The wealthy Mr. Phillips had engineered many ventures in his time, the latest being the publishing of a general-interest magazine called the *National Monthly of Canada*. He invited Emily to write for it, and some of the first issues contained excerpts from *Impressions*. Emily was soon a regular contributor to the magazine and she eventually became Women's Editor. This meant that her subject matter had to be confined to what was felt to be exclusively of interest to women, so Emily churned out articles advising on household economy, manners and fashions, home decoration, and so on; at various times in her career she used nom de plumes like "The Duchess," "Lady Jane" and "Earlie York" when writing lightweight material with which she did not want Janey Canuck identified.

Emily's protests that this innocuous fare presupposed a limited range of thought on the part of the female reader fell upon deaf ears. For the time being she had to content herself with writing articles like "Matchmaking Mammas" (by "Emilie Ferguson"): "Yes! A mother should be a matchmaker. Marriage is the most important contract in human society. If a woman desires her daughter to marry well, why should it be a crime against her, or against society, to help her in the matter? It is only the foolish and rankly hypocritical who argue to the contrary."

It was not until a few years later, after she had become Literary Editor, that Emily was able to expound on more general matters. "The Other Side of the Chinese Question" (*National Monthly,* May 1904) pleaded for a lifting of immigration restrictions on orientals wishing to enter Canada. "When we are so sparsely populated it is a grave error to exclude law abiding would-be citizens. The most serious offence against the Chinese is that they are too economical and send their wages to China."

Fifteen years later Emily, from her magisterial bench, would categorize the influx of the Chinese into Canada and the subsequent proliferation of drug trafficking and addiction as one of her major problems. But in 1904, she saw things differently. "The opium joints are little less than our whisky joints," she said. "The Chinese drink French brandy too." Noting that the Chinese were good, industrious domestics, intelligent miners, who had "no superiors as railway navvies as they can work in heat and cold," Emily maintained that Canada was afraid of the Chinaman's virtues rather than his vices.

On a fall day in 1902, Arthur was busily engaged in preparations for a big speech he was to make at Toronto's Massey Hall that evening. The reputation he had made during his tenure in England and on the Continent, as one of the Church's most eloquent speakers, had followed him home. Two thousand people were expected to pack the hall to hear him, including, of course, Emily. There was an air of keen anticipation in the Murphy household all day.

Backstage that evening the Murphys parted with an affectionate hug and Emily's excited, "Break a leg, Padre." Escorted to her seat by a church official, Emily saw the gradually filling rows of seats, the enormous stage, the elaborate frescoes and carved dadoes. The two broad, semi-circular balconies already contained few empty seats, and as she sat down with a murmur of thanks to her escort, she noted the palms, piano, rug and a row of chairs on stage, along with the ubiquitous small table and jug of water.

The group was gathering on stage—and there was Arthur, taking his seat. The rustling and coughing stopped, and the usual expectant hush before an anticipated speech took place. When the chairman had concluded his introduction, Arthur moved toward the lectern. He stumbled, recovered, and began his speech.

Emily knew something was wrong immediately. Arthur was not himself. He looked flushed. He hesitated over his words. He was not in control. Emily's heart cried out to him. What was wrong? The audience began fidgeting, coughing, rustling. He had lost them. *Stop it!* Emily wanted to shout. Can't you see he's ill? Give him a chance, you infidels! Instead she kept her gaze rigidly on her husband. He was gripping the sides of the lectern until his knuckles turned white. Somehow he got through his speech, bowed to perfunctory applause, and left the stage, his steps faltering.

Emily rushed from her seat, barely stopping to make her excuses to those occupying the remainder of the row. Backstage, Arthur had collapsed on to a couch. He was feverish, sweating and breathing hard. He mumbled something to Emily which was incoherent, and lost consciousness.

A doctor had been sent for. He arrived in a very few minutes and pronounced his diagnosis: typhoid.

An infectious bacterial disease, typhoid is caused by ingesting contaminated food or water. Toronto, then with a population of some ninety thousand, was a stinking, filthy place, where human waste was excreted on the street; sewage was piped into the lake, where it created one giant cesspool from which drinking water was drawn.[2] Outdoor privies (no more than pits in the ground) flooded the streets, and it was the custom to leave garbage uncovered, thus providing an excellent breeding ground for millions of flies.

Spitting in public was an acceptable and widely practiced activity.

It was no wonder, then, that outbreaks of typhoid, in many cases fatal, were a common occurrence. Medical treatment was still in the experimental stages, consisting of various methods of keeping the body temperature down to 102 degrees, sometimes by means of baths or cold water packs or even injections of cold water into the veins.[3]

Arthur had round-the-clock care provided by Emily and a trained nurse, and the doctor looked in twice a day. He was seriously ill. He had worked too hard without respite for too long, depleting his resistance. Emily vowed that when Arthur recovered—and she never for a moment doubted this— she would insist upon a holiday, perhaps to Manitoulin for some fishing.

For weeks Arthur hovered between life and death. The Church Parochial Mission, in dire financial straits, wrote regretting they must curtail the Mission work, and plans to send Arthur to Australia were postponed. The Murphys' financial worries, in turn, became frightening, and now the responsibility rested with Emily. The sum of five hundred dollars, which had been sent by the Mission Society, with their sympathies, was soon gone. But the *National Monthly* paid well, and wanted all the articles Emily could write, which is exactly what she gave them. She was an insomniac, which was just as well, for she found she did some of her best work after midnight. When finished for the night she would steal downstairs for a snack and a glass of milk, look in on Arthur and little Dot, and then turn in herself. The Padre was recuperating nicely, but he was still thin and weak. It would take months before he was really back on his feet and Emily prayed she would be able to keep up her flow of articles to the magazine.

Within days, however, she herself went down with the disease. She was rushed to hospital where she lay, barely conscious, for weeks. In due course Emily, too, recovered and returned, paler and thinner, to the house on Wright Avenue. As soon as she was well enough she wrote "The Diary of a Typhoid Patient," which helped pay the bills.[4]

In "Diary," which covers the period from September 16 to October 28, 1902, Emily let her mind range, fantasizing one minute, philosophizing the next. "Physical suffering is a reminder that we are tenants of the body at will, and not by right," she said. "It is the closing up of the right of way—a warning that life is lent and not given." She described how her doctor could avoid telling the truth without lying when she questioned him as to the state of her health, and how useless it was to pretend to be better if you are not. On October 16—Thanksgiving Day—she rationalized that the year had had more sun than clouds and that ugly feelings caused by four months of nursing and being nursed must be shut away.

Emily had an excellent opportunity in "Diary" to show off her classical knowledge and "encyclopedic mind." Her tendency to lard her prose with quotations from the classics, in what seemed a rather contrived fashion, could often be an irritant to the less well-versed reader. But it remained a part of her style all her life, and either you liked it or you lumped it.

The last entry in the "Diary" described her return from hospital:

There was a sortie from the front door, a precipitate attack on the ambulance—kisses, little secrets, greetings, stored-up grievances and more kisses, all in one breath. Then the big ambulance policeman carried me in. How gentle he was. Only a giant can be gentle. Tenderness is an inflection of strength. When the dwarf that attended Ivanhoe at the tournament lifted the bleeding knight he stumbled over the weight, and caused the sufferer intense pain, but the giant of the brawny arm and unconquered heart came and lifted him like a featherweight, and bore him away to a hiding place for healing and rest.

Someone was playing and singing "When Janey Canuck Comes Home." It was a homecoming that overbalanced the pain. And now the hours are a continual *Te Deum* without one *Miserere* to mar their perfect peace.

Typically, once on his feet again, Arthur had defied the advice of his doctors and begun to pick up the threads of his work again. Emily had tried to reason with him but, weak as she was, knew that it was useless. "You have been keeping us for long enough," her husband had muttered.

He accepted a post in Beeton, a tiny hamlet in the middle of nowhere about forty miles north of Toronto, and a stone's throw from the Murphy farm at Rosemont. Arthur's mother welcomed the chance to get some nourishment into her son, who was looking paler and thinner than she had ever seen him.

It was while Arthur was away on this mission that six-year-old Doris came down, in November, with a fever. When her condition continued to worsen Emily became alarmed, and a doctor was called in. The diagnosis was frightening—diphtheria—but the doctor insisted that there was no cause for concern; unless complications set in she should, with good care, be well on the way to recovery. Despite such assurances, Emily was fearful, and hardly left the child's side.

One afternoon the darkening clouds seemed more threatening than usual. The doctor was worried; complications *had* set in. Emily stayed with the child day and night, comforting her through the strangled coughs that gripped her small frame. She fought back her own tears as she watched helplessly the life draining from the little girl, who only mere days ago had been running and climbing trees in the park. Now she had to lean close to the child, for she was trying hard to say something. She was asking her mother to sing her favorite Christmas lullaby, "The Little Lord Jesus." The tears stung Emily's eyes, but she crooned the beloved song over and over, as Doris died.

Emily's grief was total. At first she refused to believe it. Then as realization sank in she withdrew, became morose, as though life had left her as well. She sent a telegram to Arthur: "DORIS JUST DIED COME MEMBRANOUS CROUP EMILY"

Arthur rushed home with the telegram still in his pocket where he had thrust it. Kathleen and Evelyn came home from school, grief-stricken. A light had gone out of the house on Wright Street, and out of the lives of those who lived there.

A sorrowful little group gathered at the village cemetery in Cookstown to watch the small white coffin lowered into the ground next to the plot where an even smaller one—carrying Madeleine—had been buried nine years before.

A heartbroken Emily wrote a little later, "Once she [Doris] worked a little motto with thread on cardboard. It contained all the ethics she had been taught—'Be Good.' Afterwards, I found this pitiful thing among her toys and had it framed."

The extent of Emily's grief and despair at Doris's death is tellingly revealed in her article for the January 1903 issue of the *National Monthly*, entitled "The Dead Child":

> "There are many kinds of sorrow," said David Harum, "but I guess that caused by the death of a child is a species by itself."
>
> The ancients used to think that the straits entering the Red Sea were very dangerous places...and they put on weeds of mourning for those who had gone [through] as though they were actually dead.
>
> And so we stand at this gate and strain our ears for a sound from the other shore, but we hear naught save the painful throbbings of our own hearts. Are they dead? Do they live? Or is it we who are dead— we who toil—we who weep—we who sin—Is it we who are dead?

The doctors now persuaded Arthur that to continue his mission work would be foolhardy. What he needed was lots of fresh air and exercise. Emily, too, needed a change of environment. An opportunity for just that suddenly presented itself. A few years earlier, Arthur had purchased a small, unsurveyed timber-limit at Jackfish Creek and Swan River, Manitoba, about two days' journey north of Winnipeg. They could go out west and live off the land!

Emily was not enamored of the idea, but they discussed it, and she "decided to compromise and go."

Her mother was horrified. "You are going to a wilderness full of foreigners and Indians!" she expostulated. Then, her voice full of grim portent, "Mark my words, Kathleen will grow up and marry an Indian!"

While Emily and the girls made their fond farewells, Arthur went out to Swan River (population 1,300) and bought a house.

The April before they left, Emily wrote one more article for the *National Monthly*. Under the byline "A Canadian" it was an adulatory biography of Sir Wilfrid Laurier, then Prime Minister. It was a remarkably fine piece, which sang his praises eloquently and certainly with every appearance of sincerity. Emily particularly admired Sir Wilfrid's firm stand on Canada's right to make her own decisions on matters affecting her relationship with Great Britain and the United States. "He refused to let Canada be entangled in Militarism," she wrote when The Boer War was in progress. "The sending of Canadian troops to South Africa is not to be regarded as a constitutional precedent, or as the fulfilment of a moral obligation... He [Laurier] maintains the best interests of Canada in relations with the United States, but with perfect justice to the Americans."

Emily sent a copy of the article to Sir Wilfrid, and he was quick to respond with a letter in his own hand:

335 Theodore, Ottawa
April 21, 1903

My dear Madam,

I have received both your letter and the article with which you have honoured me in the National Monthly.

I have read your article with great attention and, I must add, pleasure. If one fault is to be found in it it is that it is too flattering. To such a fault I can be partial.

You say that you are a Conservative. Perhaps some day you will come to Ottawa and give me the opportunity of discussing with you your political views.

With much expression of my very sincere gratitude, believe me Madam, I am,

> *Yours sincerely,*
> *Wilfrid Laurier*

During the months of waiting, Emily adjusted to the idea of leaving. "To move means a review of your whole life," she said. "Inside one little hour you laugh, swell with pride, cry, grovel with humility, and burn with indignation as the fingers of still-born projects, dead joys or foolish frolics reach out and touch you from the past... There are compensations, though. Things get cleaned up. You lose fifteen pounds of absolutely useless flesh. There is the secret and blissful consciousness of removing mountains and making things happen."

One of the first things Mrs. Murphy made happen upon her arrival in Swan River, was to become the first president of the local chapter of the Canadian Zenana Bible and Medical Society.

It was a start.

Chapter V

Janey Canuck in the West: 1903-1907

The whole land is a paradise of blossoms... How unfortunate one is to live in the older provinces! Existence there is only canned life. We of the West belong to "the few elect."

Settlers had been pouring into the Canadian West since the waning years of the 1800s, a stampede which was to continue for the remainder of the next decade. Many of the settlers came to work land they had bought during the real estate boom of 1882, but most were newcomers, emigrants from Europe in the hundreds and thousands, of many different nationalities, religions and backgrounds, each seeking to prosper in a land rich with the promise of a good life for an honest day's work.

As they swarmed across the prairies, staking their claims and putting down their roots, the sleeping land from Manitoba westward awoke to receive them, and settlements shot up almost overnight. Emily and Arthur were a part of this transformation, and Emily recorded their travels in a collection of essays entitled *Janey Canuck in the West,* published in 1910.

This was a time when Canadians were eager to read about what was happening in their country. The population explosion produced a demand for books which could not be satisfied by the few presses already in existence. New publishing houses sprang up to fill the need, and an air of excitement surrounded the new growth. Emily began her writing career, therefore, when publishers were clamoring for material, and she was writing the kind they, and the reading public, wanted. It was virtually an insatiable market.

In the late afternoon of a summer day in 1903, the Murphy family boarded the *Athabasca.*

"It is a big flit we are taking," Emily wrote. "The moisture in my eyes is purely the result of smoke from the engines. Blessed old Toronto, the home of our love! You have been good to us. I cannot forbear kissing my hands to your charm and beauty. To live with you is to be happy ever after."

On the *Athabasca* the Murphys met a Scotsman whose hobby was the tabulation of all kinds of facts relating to Canada. "He has noted," said a seasick-prone Emily, "that in the years 1870 to 1902 the deaths on Canadian and British sea-going vessels, in our waters, have been 5,247. We have been trying to figure out the chances against our landing safely. They are, we conclude, about 100,000 to 1."

Emily had her first look at a grain elevator in Port Arthur, where the great bulk of grain grown in the Northwest was stored. As might be expected, it was a thorough inspection, producing both admiration and some instant advice for the Motherland on the importance of Canadian wheat to the Empire. "It is," she said, "on these great mountains of grain that the federation of the Empire will largely stand. Interdependent, the Colony shall feed the Motherland and in return shall receive protection against the covetous claws of the world."

Winnipeg was obviously responsible for the beginning of Emily's bewitchment by the West:

> How the sun shines here in Winnipeg! One drinks it in like wine. And how the bells ring! It is a town of bells and light set in a blaze of gold. Surely the West *is* golden—the sky, flowers, wheat, hearts.
>
> Winnipeg is changing from wood to stone. She is growing city-like in granite and asphalt. Hitherto, banks and hotels were run up overnight, and had to pay for themselves in the next twenty-four hours.
>
> Winnipeg has something western, something southern, something quite her own. She is an up-and-doing place. She has swagger, impelling arrogance, enterprise, and an abiding spirit of usefulness.
>
> "What I like," says an American to me, "is the eternal spunk of the place."
>
> On the streets of Winnipeg, there are people who smile at you in English, but speak in Russian. There are rushful, pushful people from "the States," stiff-tongued Germans, ginger-headed Icelanders, Galicians, Norwegians, Poles, and Frenchmen, all of whom are rapidly becoming irreproachably Canadian. In all there are sixty tongues in the pot.
>
> The real Westerner is well proportioned. He is tall, deep-chested, and lean in the flank. His body betrays, in every poise and motion, a daily life of activity in the open air. His glances are full of wist and warmth. There is an air of business about his off-hand way of settling a matter that is very assuring.
>
> Every mother's son of them is a compendium of worldly wisdom and a marvel of human experience. What more does any country want?

A few days later the Murphys left for "Poplar Bluff" (Emily's fictitious name for Swan River), a two day journey north by train. The millions of sunflowers they passed, in one continuous bed, were cause for comment, and when Emily brought them up in conversation with a fellow passenger —a Scot—he proceeded to astonish her with a litany of their many uses.[1]

At Portage-la-Prairie and Dauphin the conductor accommodatingly waited while they had dinner and tea, there being no Pullman or dining car on the train, and at midnight, "After two wretched days and two equally wretched nights of travelling," they reached Swan River—to find their trunks were missing. Being assured they would come on the next train, three days hence, they went in search of a hotel. There was not much choice. The one they picked as being the least offensive offered them a room with "a sad-colored carpet, the smallest washstand ever seen outside a doll's house, and a looking glass that distorted our faces." It was also insect ridden.

The food was terrible, inclining Emily to the opinion that "There is nothing viler than 'good plain Canadian fare.' No, nothing." But before she went to bed that night she had learned that "Manitoba is a corruption of two Indian words, *Manitou napa*, 'the land of the great spirit,' translated more freely by the Manitobans as 'God's Country.'"

An outing the next day to a neighboring village acclimatized Emily to the autumn flower-covered trails, alive with rabbits. "Hitchy, twitchy, munchy things they are. The Indians call them *wahboos*, which means 'the little white chaps.'" Stopping at the village hotel for refreshments, the party ordered milk and biscuits, but Emily insisted upon a ruddy port "that harboured a kiss and reflected a glance." She drank a little more than one glass "and enjoyed the unusual delight of *feeling* wicked that is only experienced by innocent people."

The first day of September came, and with it the opening of the duck shooting season. Despite her lack of enthusiasm for the sport, Emily did some practice shooting, but failed to impress Arthur, who assured her that the fact she kept her eyes closed the whole time made no appreciable difference to her aim, so not to worry about it.

The lack of fruit bothered Emily quite a bit, so she was forced to substitute vegetables. Climbing over a fence one day to pull a yellow turnip, she noticed there were geese in the field. Emily was afraid of geese. "They honk, and squawk, and quack, and hiss, and the more I *shoo* them with my skirts, the worse they are." In her attempts to clamber back over the fence away from the feathered tormentors she stirred up the animosity of a wasp and the situation was saved in the nick of time by Arthur, who used his hat to cut short the insect's ill-mannered career. The turnip was worth the effort. Apart from its distinctive flavor, which Emily was very partial to, it was, according to her, unrivalled as a complexion beautifier: "It acts on the skin like magic. When anyone declines to eat a raw turnip, it is a sure sign that he or she has grown old."

That same day they bought a yoke of oxen, for 150 dollars, and got their money's worth in fun during the purchase:

> The owner, a queer codger with a red, bibulous face, was anxious to place the good traits of the animals before us in the most favorable light, but in putting the oxen through their paces would burst into purple patches of vituperation.

"Go on, you blankety-blank, knock-kneed, cloven-hoofed chewer of cuds!

"Now, ma'am, can't they walk some?

"Get out of the mud there, you stall-fed, lounging lump of wickedness!

"Yes, siree, Boss! You needn't laugh. Them's the finest beasts in the valley. They're slick as shootin'."

I suspect it is true what they say out here: "No one can serve God and drive oxen."

The stores in Swan River were crammed with everything one could possibly want to buy, including blue and gold souvenir glassware decorated with the picture of the barber's shop, hotel and butcher's stall. Property changed hands daily between villagers and newcomers with the loan companies egging them on. Real estate offices opened in livery stables, with people making one hundred dollars a day on land they had never seen.[2]

Despite the plentiful supply of clergy (five ministers plus students from theological colleges on summer assignments), the village had a serious problem no amount of money or spiritual comfort could cure: it was a costly and difficult place in which to keep clean. "Circumstances," said Emily, "are not calculated to encourage the great unwashed. The only soft water available is caught in rain barrels. About every fifth family has a well, and about every fifth well is usable... Some of the households drink the water that drips from their refrigerators. This is considered the best— *No. 1 Hard,* so to speak."

The Murphy house had no laths or plaster on the walls; apparently, there were no plasterers in Swan River:

> The paper is put on over stretched cheese-cloth, and every time you lean against it, you go through and see daylight in the chinks of the outer shell. The men are at work doing better things for us. We shall have three bedrooms, a dressing room, parlour, study, dining room, kitchen, and servant's room. We have no furnace, bathroom, cellar, or woodshed. Perhaps we shall have these later, for the rule here seems to be to build from the top. The stone foundation is usually built after the house has been standing a year; later a cellar is dug out, and finally, as the family increases in wealth, or as they get leisure, a drain is added.

On a day "brimful of liquid sunshine," Arthur bought her a pony, "a mongrel Indian pony," which Emily promptly christened Shawna, or, in Indian, "Sweet Thing." She came to believe, though, that he might be better named Paul, "Because he suffers not a woman to have authority. He fairly bowls along with the Padre, but once I mount he stands stock still."

The Murphys had problems with the oxen, and with the workmen giving whisky to the Indians, resulting in death by fire and attempted murder. Bears were frequent visitors to the village and other animals, large and small, abounded. But over all, it was the Northern Lights which made the greatest impression. Words to describe them failed even Emily, the best she could come up with being, "An intermediate, somewhat between a thought and a thing." The children did better, naming them "glory gleams."

It was around this time that Emily tackled the attainment of her lifelong ambition: the making of a pie. "All I knew about a pie hitherto, was to know it when I saw it. But now!"

The first crust was not a success. Nor were several succccding ones. At first, the pastry was "tough enough to sew buttons on;" some boggy mixtures followed which the family called "muskegs." They ribbed Emily unmercifully, saying that she had proved the falsity of the dictum that it was not possible to eat your pie and have it, and so on. Emily took it in good humor, and persisted. Her greatest difficulty came in decorating the edges. Having tried several devices, none of which satisfied her, she asked her sympathetic friend and counsellor, the milkman. He had no opinion to offer, apparently, but told her an unforgettable story of one of his customers who, in the same difficulty, sought the advice of her servant, Bridget, who always produced magnificently decorated pies.

"Why, indade Mum," replied Bridget, "I do it with your false teeth."

One day Emily and Arthur set out to inspect their timber-limit. The thermometer stood at forty-eight degrees below zero, and Emily was bundled into the sleigh on a heap of hay, rugs, furs and pillows. They travelled along beaten trails and across snow fields. The horses were rimey with frozen breath and Emily found the cutter uncomfortable after a while. "It has not enough back or side support, and there is not sufficient room to stretch your legs. The seat is too big for one, and not large enough for two. It is provocative of rheumatism and kidney disease," she complained. At one point, she emerged from her "nest" to hold the horses while Arthur took a shot at a coyote. He missed. Later in their journey, Arthur spied a moose hurtling along the trail ahead of them. He was too late with his gun, much to Emily's delight, for she considered the moose to be "God's own horses," which prompted Arthur to accuse her of moralizing, and to embark on a lengthy dissertation on the subject of moose and their habits.

At seven o'clock that night they sighted the Doukhobor village of Vosne-senia and went straight to the house of Eli, who frequently worked for them. The village, built on rising ground, had perfect drainage. Ditches on either side of the village carried the water to a small creek that wound through the lowland. The houses were arranged on both sides of a wide street, one-storied, of unsawn lumber plastered with clay. They were whitewashed and frescoed with vivid dadoes. Some had verandas ornamented with carving. Blinds, made of several layers of hemp, were on the outside.

The Murphys were warmly welcomed for the night. Four generations of men, women and children gathered around them, examining them with a directness that Emily found a little disconcerting. They took off her headgear, fur coat, golf jacket and, finally, her footgear. Then they all laughed at the mountain of clothing she had shed. Her hatpins afforded them considerable amusement, and they took turns in pushing them in and out of her cap. The Murphys had brought their own food, and Emily was given free rein in the kitchen to prepare it. There was some repartee, if you could call it that, when Emily was cooking the bacon. The vegetarian Doukhobors wrinkled their noses at "the stank," and there ensued an abortive discussion on the subject of "making graveyards of your stomachs" (Eli), and the Israelites eating angel food in the wilderness but not profiting by it (Emily).

The news had spread that there were visitors in the village, and soon the house was full of curious townsfolk. Emily was envious of the colorful and comfortable garments the womenfolk wore, "even blending purple, red and green in a happy triple alliance," and "their bodies are not jails of bones and steels, and they wear no cotton-batting contrivances," she sighed.

An evening of music followed, before everyone retired for the night. The Murphy bed consisted of "a feather mattress as soft as marshmallows, and a heap of pillows and blankets. The mattress was very short, being calculated to accommodate only the body and not the legs. It was laid on a wooden bench which was about five feet wide, and ran nearly all the way round the room." Emily spent a restless night in suffocating heat, for the women kept piling on dry tamarack wood at intervals through the night, and the cat, who had fallen in love with her for feeding it some meat earlier on, spent the night walking all over her.

Breakfast, which consisted of a soup made of cabbages, onions, potatoes and butter, played havoc with the tastebuds of the visitors. "A raw onion is palatable," said Emily, "a cooked onion is toothsome, but an onion that has merely undergone a heat change is devastating in its effects upon the feeder." The meal was followed by an introduction to the domestic arts in which all the Doukhobor women were skilled.

Emily learned that, years before, the womenfolk had taken over the hard labor when their fathers, sons and husbands were exiled to Siberia. Indeed, they still did much of the heavy work in the fields as well as their spinning, knitting, basket-weaving and linen-making. "By unfriendly critics," said Emily, "much has been made of the fact that the Doukhobor women perform the arduous work of harnessing themselves to the plough, but this is entirely at their own suggestion." These women were housewives who did not believe that their homes were jails with their babies as the turnkeys. "On the other hand," said Emily, "she is not expected, as our women are, to be a combination of Mary, Martha, Magdalen, Bridget and the Queen of Sheba."

The Murphys were about to leave when Emily learned that in one of the houses the women were making linseed oil, and she was determined to watch the process. The flax had been chopped and the women were kneading the meal in troughs, which was then heated in a large shallow pan and subjected to great pressure under a jack-screw. The refuse, after the oil was extracted, was given to cows, but the children, too, licked it up greedily. The Doukhobors used the oil for various purposes, but mainly for cooking, in the place of animal fats.

"I am convinced," said Emily, "that these people from the shores of the Black Sea will make excellent citizens. They do not steal—or very seldom—fight, drink intoxicants, smoke or swear. Their lives are saturated with ideas of thrift and small economies. They hold themselves slaves of neither priest nor landlord, and their history is a story of sturdy struggling for independence." According to Emily, only a small percentage of Doukhobors took part in the controversial pilgrimages "to find Christ," and those who did were duped into it. But this did not prevent their detractors from proclaiming their unfitness as settlers. All in all, Emily saw much to approve of in the Doukhobor way of life, regarding them not so much as fanatics but as "Baptists gone to seed" (in the words of American author Elbert Hubbard who visited the Doukhobors around the same time as the Murphys).

However, Emily forecast a threatening future for the Doukhobors. The land which the Government had allotted to them was being thrown open to new settlers who badly needed it. Emily worried that the traditions and principles to which the Doukhobors had adhered for so many generations would "be whittled down by the jack-knife of all-pervading expediency," as their members applied for homesteads. "Their little Arcadias will be broken up and presently their women, too, will be affecting hatpins, corsets, and yellow garters. The pity of it!"

It was growing dusk when the Murphys left Vosnesenia for the next stage on the journey northward: the Doukhobor sawmill. They were now in Saskatchewan and the road cut by the Doukhobors was an excellent one, marked out by mile posts. It was dark, the cold was biting, and the snow crunched as the sleigh passed over it. Emily cuddled deeper into her blankets, and conversation was at a premium. Arthur tried some poetry. "With how sad steps, O Moon! thou climbst the skies. How silently, and with how wan a face." Emily accused him of showing off, but it only served to produce another quote, this time from Emerson on the creation of light, after which they both went into Shelley, followed by "a hot discussion of Bacon's theory that all life is larger and more vigorous upon the full of the moon."

It was at this stage in their conversation that Arthur decided to broach the subject of Emily's lack of observance of Sundays; she should, he said, teach Sunday school instead of making pies—and so on. That started them on another conversational joust which lasted until they reached the sawmill at eight o'clock. "I did not know," wrote Emily, "that I was cold until I got into the heat. Had anyone touched me, I would have broken in two. Any fool can travel, but it takes a wise woman not to." After some hot tea and food, Emily prepared her bed on a large bench. The men slept at the far end. There were no washing facilities.

Emily awoke at four o'clock, slipped on her moccasins, mittens and cap and stole out into the night. "Rabbits and prairie chickens were gambolling about the yard in a risky frisky fashion. The Doukhobors do not take life, and so these furtive wood-folk have become domesticated." She followed a light in a building a little way off, and, curious, peeped in. It was the stable, warm, clean, and cosy.

She was awakened shortly after eight o'clock by the sound of a man turning a grindstone. Soon the camp foreman took her on a tour; she wished she had taken him up on his offer of a bed in his quarters, which included what we would today call a sauna. After breakfast Arthur took her to see the hay which was awaiting transportation to their limit. The Doukhobors, who had the contract for hauling it in, were efficient and, with a few exceptions, scrupulously honest and trustworthy.

For the last leg of their journey, "The Padre wrapped me up snugly...I was the first woman, white black or red, to traverse this part of Canada, and he was anxious that I should establish a good precedent."

After two hours' travel, Emily's feet, despite being wrapped in three pairs of stockings and moosehide moccasins lashed with leather thongs, were freezing. Arthur tried to light the lantern to use as a foot warmer, but the oil had frozen and refused to ignite. "He was relentless," Emily grumbled. "I had to get out, then and there, and walk." She found it hard to walk in all her clothes, on the uneven ground, where the sharp, freshly-cut roots hurt her feet, and trying to keep up with the horses (and Arthur) did nothing to improve her temper. She was furious with Arthur but had to admit that she was getting warmer, and when she saw one of her own blue streamers fluttering in a moose-willow, it put all thoughts of being hateful to him out of her head. She had made these streamers and Andrew, one of their Indian woodsmen, had blazed the trees with them to mark the trail which would otherwise have been obliterated by the first fall of snow.

Emily reminded herself of Andrew's strategy to avoid getting lost in the woods. "He always selects a high object far ahead in the direction he wishes to go," she said, "and travels toward it. The lack of this precaution is why men who are lost in the forest travel in a circle."

Over mile upon mile of muskeg they travelled, "...desolation without sublimity and barrenness without relief. A land bitter raw and utterly worthless." Toward evening they came into heavier timber again, chiefly poplar with the occasional jackpine. The timber wolves were in full cry. Emily, who had been seeing moving shadowy forms in the dusk wherever she looked, calculated she had spent nine hours in the open sleigh with the temperature fifty degrees below zero. She was sleepy. Oh, for a comfortable warm bed after some fine hot food and drink!

"Wake up, Cookie!" Arthur's voice pierced her drowsiness. "This is our log road, and these are all your own trees, miles of them. Look up, sweetheart!"

They had entered a forest of towering, spear-headed spruces, but try as she would Emily could not keep her eyes open long enough to take them in. She was stiffening with cold, her teeth chattering like castanets. Arthur tried to get her to drink some brandy, but her lips froze to the metal of the flask. But a few twists more of the road and then, glory be! Voices! Two lumberjacks lifted her out of the sleigh and into a wide, low cabin, bright and warm, where the smell of fresh wheaten bread assailed them, and a man negotiated "pots and pans with the air of one conducting a religious ceremony."

They had arrived at the camp.

"I slept the sleep of the well-fed and woke up twice as good as new," wrote Emily. Her bed, a moss-lined chest, had been "stiff, angular, ugly within and uglier without, but this nest of logs in the northern wilds has a motherly suggestion about it that is irresistible." And indestructible: "Nature may bring all her big guns to bear upon it, but without avail."

After breakfast, there being no sign of Arthur, Emily decided to go for a ride. She got her saddle out of the sleigh and adjusted it to a bronco that belonged to the foreman. As she tightened the girths, Emily had some misgivings. "She had a calico-coloured hide, and a bad, red eye. Her ribs were flat, her hips cat-hammed, and her tail looked like a used-up shaving brush. Her nose, too, was sufficiently pronounced to declare the most stubborn propensities."

But, muttering, "Nothing venture, nothing win," Emily swung into the saddle—and into the unexpected.

The bronco "curved her back up in the middle like a one-humped camel, plumped down behind and reared in front, at the same time keeping her legs as stiff as stilts. She appeared to be three parts rubber and the rest iron." Emily was shaken to the core. Her hair parted from its pins, falling down her back and into her face. At home, when her own horse bucked, Emily would hit him between the ears with her whip. She tried it now "on this flying bunch of sinews," and was flung unceremoniously to the ground before she knew what had happened.

Unhurt but furious, Emily tried to whip the poor beast into submission until the cook came running over wringing his hands "in an ecstasy of woe." "She keel you," he wailed. "I know she weel. The Padre, he keel me. He keel me dade." With the cook's help, and with her hair re-pinned, Emily remounted and found Dinah ("short for dynamite, I suppose") more tractable, but still uninclined to go anywhere. The contest was declared a draw, and Emily was forbidden to ride the bronco again as "she was not broken to skirts."

In the camp, Emily learned how to discern the survey lines, talked with the skinners, joined in their singsongs, and ate fried pork, bread, butter, tea and syrup with them. As she once said, "I get transcendent delight from eating." She also enjoyed watching the birds, particularly the Whisky Jack (so named because he chases around the wine cup). But Emily soon set about learning the business of working the timber.

In the first stage, the foreman blazed the trees to be cut, and the men, in pairs, chopped them. When the tree fell, the swampers lopped off the branches and the sawyers divided it into logs. There were from two to five logs in a tree, and a log, Emily discovered, was about as thick as she was tall, and about twelve feet in length. Fortunately, the men were expert: "Nikolai can drop a big spruce as deftly as a fly is cast. It falls just in the spot he says it will."

The skidders were the men who rolled the logs up a spiked incline by means of canthooks. It was dangerous work, but the men were "strong, supple, and active as cats." The logs were then piled up on the heavy sleighs like loads of hay, and taken to the dump. Here they were stamped, and piled on huge skidways to await the break-up of the ice, at which point they would be rolled into the river "to start on their troublesome career southward."

Emily's stay at the camp was coming to an end, but not before she had the opportunity (thanks to Henri, the French-Canadian interpreter) of meeting and talking with the local Indians, mainly Crees and Chippewas. Emily shared to a great extent the traditional views that white society in general held then toward the Indians and other indigenous peoples, but she gained a respect for the skill and the independence of these native Canadians that tempered her otherwise rough judgments.

A leisurely Sunday evening round the cookhouse stove enabled Emily to catch up with her writing, and listen in on some of the conversation which drifted along in that easy, languid manner which is customary with people resting after hours spent in outdoor exercise.

On Monday morning they left, Emily with some reluctance:

> I was homesick leaving. I hold those in high esteem who live under green trees. The life is large, fine and sane. It clears the mind of many mists, and teaches one the fundamental facts of life.
>
> There is a sense of isolation in the woods that you do not find to be loneliness. A large part of the pleasure, too, is to discover that you can not only live without the modern conveniences and amusements of the city, but that also you are really happier without them. It gives you a wondrous sense of satisfaction with yourself.

The Murphys soon stopped at another Doukhobor village, Traitzkor, and Emily's garments were again examined with interest by the women. But this time Emily reciprocated some of the criticism. The Doukhobor women, she noted, had no hair to speak of, a direct result of the continuous wearing of kerchiefs, which has an injurious effect upon the scalp. In return for being allowed to try on their headgear, Emily doled out some strongly flavored cough drops which caused quite a stir as they were passed from mouth to mouth. A bottle of eau-de-cologne which she also gave them, was not a success, the Doukhobors regarding such affectation as sinful.

Emily was quick to observe that "Every house in the village has a swinging cradle, and in every cradle there is a baby. Philanthropists, preachers, and socialists who are working themselves into a fine frenzy over the decline of the birthrate would find here their ideal." Emily, whose own figure had filled out to a matronly rotundness, mused on the way home about the difference in standards between the two societies. One revered the robust and fertile female, while the other paid homage to "the raw-boned, gaunt muscled woman of the Gibson creation, incapable of having children."

Sometimes Arthur would be away from home for weeks at a time, developing plans for his timber-limit. He had brought with him the same determination to succeed that had made him a brilliant preacher, but he had much to learn about his new life, and the first months were troubled ones financially. Soon, however, he became more expert at timber-cruising and even showed a facility for outwalking the Indians. Gradually the money started to come in. The Murphy fortune was further enhanced when, swept up in the real estate fever, Arthur, with some partners, bought eight thousand acres of land around Carrot River in Saskatchewan at seven dollars an acre, selling it soon after for double the price.[3]

With the girls, now in their teens, at Havergal College in Winnipeg, Emily was left alone a great deal. Not that one could ever be truly "alone" with housekeeper Caroline: "A most fearful and wonderful conversationalist. She can talk for hours without stopping. It does not matter if you do not listen. She is content to supply the questions and answers herself." On one occasion Caroline outdid herself. At a loose end for some juicy gossip, she spread the word that "Mrs. Murphy wuz expectin' a little addition to the family in the Spring." Her tenure after this unjustified remark was destined to be shortlived.

Emily was reviewing books for the *Winnipeg Tribune* and enjoying it tremendously. The twenty or so books that arrived every month by train soon filled all the available shelves and table tops in her study. She wrote during the day and into the night, and as each book was reviewed, cut out the published notice and pasted it into the back of the book. She continued to send her articles to the *National Monthly,* and was also beginning to be noticed by other magazines and periodicals as well.

During this time, "Votes for Women" had become a catchphrase. Although it had few supporters—even among the female ranks—the idea was beginning to take hold. There was, however, considerable opposition. A statement made in 1906 by Grover Cleveland, former U.S. president, summed up the tone of hostility: "We all know how much further women go than men in their social rivalries and jealousies. Sensible and responsible women do not want to vote. The relative positions to be assumed by man and woman in the working out of our civilization were assigned long ago by a higher intelligence than ours."

"Sensible and responsible" women like Emily's contemporary, Nellie McClung, teacher, writer and outspoken feminist, were in fact, beginning to be heard in the West. Soon Emily would be adding her voice to theirs, eventually leading the chorus, on the printed page, on the podium, and in the offices of power, pushing for changes in the laws which likened the female half of the adult population to idiots, lunatics and criminals.[4]

For now, Emily was committed to making the Murphys' new life work. She did much of the bookkeeping for the timber-limits and the planning and purchasing of supplies in Winnipeg. She became expert in lumberjacks' outfits, moccasins, rubber boots, shirts and so forth, and her fondness for stockpiling stores in large amounts—the family was always teasing her about her siege mentality—proved invaluable. She was in her element buying quarters of beef, sacks of rolled oats, barrels of sugar, sacks of potatoes, crates of condensed milk (lumberjacks called it "tinned cow"), tubs of butter, pails of lard, and much more. "They keep open house in the camp," she wrote, "to the music of knives and forks."

In becoming totally involved in her new community and her family's place in it, she could put the past behind her and become strong again. Emily Murphy had an inner strength and common sense that no amount of outward clowning could mask. That same strength which had enabled her to deal in her own way with the ultimate tragedy of losing a beloved child would serve her well in the face of future hardships.

Spring came and with it the chance to get on horseback and ride into the woods. Whenever they could, Emily and the girls did so, and, having seen the ice move out of the river, relinquished forever the sobriquet "tenderfeet." They were hereafter entitled to be called "sourdoughs."

"The pressure of the ice on its downward career was terrific," wrote Emily. "It swept out part of the log dam and tore from the river bed the huge spruce piles that held the booms, as though they were inconsequential toothpicks." The ice having moved out, now was the time to wet a line for pike. Locally known as "Jack fish," they had at this time of year left their lairs and were heading up river "as though making a direct trail for the North Pole." They were hungry, and swallowed a bare hook greedily. Emily cast her line one April morning and almost instantaneously her cork disappeared, and she was almost pulled off the bank. She was sure it was a shark at least. Arthur was equally excited. "You've *got* him," he shouted.

"But how am I going to *git* him?" Emily shrieked back.

Arthur sent a bullet zipping through the water, but still Emily couldn't pull her catch to shore. Arthur seized her rod in an attempt to help her. In her excitement, Emily grabbed a net and jumped on to a big log boom to try and capture her prize—and went straight into the water.

"When the Padre got me on the bank again," she wrote, "he dropped me with what I considered unnecessary violence."

"And now, *madam*," he said, "for the future you will *much* oblige me by thinking twice, thinking thrice, thinking *several* times before you attempt to walk a floating log."

"I would rather be drowned than saved in so hateful a fashion," fumed Emily. "Writers of fiction do not tell the truth about these thrilling rescues."

Arthur dissolved into mighty laughter at the black and wrathful looks he got from Emily and derisively presented her with a wreath of honor made from willows. "Ugh!" she said, "I could fairly eat him."

Long walks in the woods were a constant delight to Emily, who communed with nature like a born and bred countrywoman. Gophers, birds, flowers, all came under her scrutiny, and she had much to say, and quote, about them all. With Arthur away so much, Emily quickly assumed responsibility for running the seventeen horses and five men who worked their farm for them.

Caroline had been replaced by new "baggage," who apparently cooked well, except on Sundays, when she asserted with religious fervor that cold "vittals" must be the order of the day, much to Emily's dissatisfaction. No amount of cajolery, threats or verbal blows moved this kitchen autocrat, with the result that every Sunday there were secret plots to overcome the tyranny, for "We would rather take [such abuse] than sweep, cook, and burn our fingers," Emily admitted.

That summer the girls and Emily had their first close encounter with a bear. They were walking home with a runaway mare they had captured, and had stopped to pick mushrooms and saskatoon berries when a huge bear with three cubs emerged from the brush within a few yards of them. They flew for their lives leaving a long trail of cat-tails, golden-rod, peas, snakeroot and mushrooms in their wake. They stopped running at the first farmhouse, where they caught their breath and drank unlimited quantities of buttermilk.

"The Padre," said Emily, "is getting conceited in the extreme about his prowess as a hunter." And with good reason. He had shot and killed his first moose that winter, then a fox, and claimed his first bear shortly afterward. It happened when he and his guide, ranging timber up north, were surprised at their supper by a large female bear attracted by the irresistible odor of the food. On her second foray around their lean-to, she came within easy range and Arthur's second bullet felled her. "Her head was placed in a tree to dry," says Emily, "but the next morning when the coast was clear, her cubs climbed up and ate it."

While Emily was apt to rhapsodize about her beloved West during the summers ("The climate is like wine, without its headache. Ah! I am a drunken tippler"), there were times in the winters when she hated the snow

With daughters Kathleen and Evelyn in 1906

and the isolation of her new home. "All the world seems to have come to a full stop," she said one night, when she was the only one up in a sleeping household. She listened to the wolves howl and longed for the "sweet security of streets, the pushing crowds, the call of the latest editions, the velvety sweep of feet, the whir of the automobile, the glare of the stage, the long rows of houses, and all else that once I hated." Emily found herself agreeing with the Indians that "Heaven is in the south."

As she looked out of her window, the only light she could see, winking in the distance across the river, was the new little Victorian Order Hospital on the hill, which she had helped to bring to Swan River, marking her first community project. She had been proud to become the first president of its Board of Control.

Another servant joined their household that winter, and the Sunday "cold vittals" became an unmourned memory. "Anna is an ignorant, wasteful, dish-breaking Swede, who is worse than useless," snapped Emily. "She translates 1/4 teaspoon into 14, and wonders how apples can get into dumplings."

Anna, who usually seemed to be suffering from one kind of pain or other, often wore bloodstained rags on her fingers, which she always seemed to be cutting. And she was eccentric too. One evening at supper the family searched in vain for the bread. Later, when Anna had returned from a prayer meeting, it was revealed that the bread had been in her bed getting warm! Needless to say, the rapid turnover in domestic help in the Murphy household continued.

The Murphys stayed in Swan River for four years until, once again, Arthur sought new pastures. "There is no use arguing with him, threatening, or beseeching him," Emily said, "He is going to fold up his tents and steal away. He wants to have a look at Edmonton, and I am to look at it too."

Their train, which was three hours late, left Swan River at five on a May morning in 1907.

Chapter VI

Edmonton—A New Life: 1907-1916

Never belittle the argument of an opponent.

Alberta had been a province for two years by 1907, and Edmonton, with a population of about eighteen thousand expanding at a rate of thirty percent every year, was its fastest growing city. Men outnumbered women, young outnumbered old, newcomers outnumbered natives, and horses outnumbered everyone. True, there might be a handful of cars, but Edmonton streets were clogged by horse traffic of one kind or another. There were strings of pack horses, smart horses pulling smart surreys, horses pulling covered wagons and fire engines, and supporting mounted policemen; teams and wagons filled the market square. Edmonton literally moved on horseback.

Settlers from Asia, Europe, Britain, the U.S. and Scandinavia chattered along the wooden sidewalks. Overalls, workshirts and buckskin jackets jostled the more simply dressed, and hobbleskirted females in ornate hats elbowed their counterparts in shawls. Cleanshaven men were rare, and if a man didn't take his tobacco in a cigar or pipe he chewed it or snuffed it.

Mills and brickyards provided Edmonton with building material and the coal mined along the river kept it warm. There were fourteen churches, two flour mills, three grain elevators, several lumber and brickyards, a pork packing plant, a woollen mill, three English language newspapers and three theatres. Commerce and real estate flourished.[1]

This was the Edmonton in which Emily was to spend the remainder of her life.

The Murphys took the train north across the muskeg, breakfasted at Erwood, where the ice was still on the river, got off the train at Star City ("In the West seven houses make a city"), bought a rifle, engaged a team and driver and started across country for Melfort.

Suddenly the horses, in crossing a creek, which was in flood, struck a hole and went into twelve feet of water. ("The seats, valises, robes, gun, and coats went downstream, but the Padre held on to me, all the while warning me in excited gasps not to get excited.") The Murphys got to shore safely, if somewhat wet. They rescued some of their belongings further down stream where the flood had carried them to shore, and took refuge in a nearby farmhouse where they were given fresh warm clothing, tea and hot whisky. At Melfort they picked up the train again and, after stopovers at Prince Albert and Warman Junction, arrived in Edmonton.

It did not take Emily long to discover that the people of Edmonton were socially inclined. "There is much tea and tennis, golf, 'mobiling, dancing, dining and wild riding around the hills," and...paper chases! In *Janey Canuck in the West* she describes a paper chase, which was the Edmontonian alternative to riding with hounds. Emily was riding Goldenrod, a big yellow Irish hunter, "A rare equine unification of fire and steel that always keeps me dubious as to my mastership of him." She rode astride, as most of the women did. "It is safer, more comfortable, more healthful and in every way consistent with good taste. Besides, here is the wide and tolerant West; everyone knows that a woman's boots are not pinned to her skirts."

The "hares," who took a discreet course over previously constructed hurdles, got a start of three minutes—and the hunt was on. Following the paper, "The horses slip, stretch, strain and gasp, but never shirk. It is the dry air and altitude—and the quality known as grit—that sweeps these superb creatures up the incline: for here, in this land of daylight and sunshine, no-one ever heard of a winded horse."

A spread-eagle field had lost the trail in yellow stubble but Dr. Ferris recovered it. "It was bound to be a Ferris, for there are four of them riding today. Irish blood is sure to show when it comes to a run 'cross country." The pace was fierce, setting the brain in a whirl and transfixing every sensory nerve. "We skirt a sleugh, cross a meadow, take a stream, miss the paper, find it, and are out on the highway." Mrs. Pardee, Catherine Henderson and Capt. Jack O'Neil Hayes pressed for the lead by setting a heartbreaking pace.

Emily did not make the finish. Goldenrod swerved suddenly and could not be cajoled or coaxed to follow the others. "I hit him for the first time," said Emily. "I hit him hard, and then the saddle slid to his haunches. The girth was broken, and that is why he swerved. There is no doubt of it. Goldenrod will be an angel long before me." Once again, Emily had reacted impulsively and regretted it, a characteristic she never quite overcame. When she returned to the Golf Club, having mended the girth with her garters, small groups with frightened faces were discussing an accident. Several riders had collided, including the Master of the Meet, and were lying unconscious and severely injured. The hunt broke up in sadness.

The Murphys bought a house on 12th Street, in the south end of the city, and lived in it until 1916.[2]

Arthur was trying his hand at prospecting for coal; Emily was less enthusiastic about the venture, but she often accompanied him (principally to hold on to the back of the trap, acting as a brake, when they plunged down steep inclines, and also to strain her neck watching for survey lines). It was rough going, particularly when the price of coal dropped from five to three dollars a ton while the cost of mining it rose with every foot drilled. But for a while their investment paid off, and the Murphys were mining 150 tons of coal a day from their Rosedale mine and selling it throughout the province.

Adversity came one morning when their mine foreman discovered water to within twenty feet of the top of the shaft. Fifty feet of water had poured in over night. Arthur set two pumps to work for two weeks, but failed to budge the water. Government authorities condemned the mine. It was a blow. It was also a mystery until they realized that it was the river, which had entered the mine through an underground opening, they had been trying to pump out! Arthur calculated that the experience had cost them one hundred thousand dollars, but he was not deterred. He bought another mine with fifteen miles of coal, one mile wide, along Lake Wabamum, about fifty miles from Edmonton, and sold it a few years later for a handsome profit, which he took in real estate instead of cash. During these boom days many people were making and losing fortunes in land speculation, and Arthur was no exception. Emily worried from time to time, but mostly took it in stride.

They were heady days, consisting of rides out to inspect the mine (with the girls joining them on their own mounts), weekly home gatherings at which Emily entertained her fast growing circle of friends, and dinner parties that became the talk of the town. Much as she loved the north woods and country life, Emily had missed the entertaining, the dressing up, and social intercourse of urban life.

Horseback-riding with the girls

A woman by the name of Nellie McClung was making a name for herself on the subjects of the female franchise and Prohibition (she favored both), as were other women. Alice Jamieson followed Emily in becoming a police court magistrate in Calgary; Louise Crummy McKinney was fighting for temperance and Henrietta Muir Edwards for the plight of women and children; Irene Marryat Parlby, a visitor from England, stayed to become the champion of the farm worker and of legislation for education, health and child welfare, and a cabinet minister to boot.

The movement for the enfranchisement of women, begun in the U.S. by Susan B. Anthony some years before, and taken up by Emmeline Pankhurst among others in Great Britain, was catching fire and moving abroad. The newspapers were full of accounts of outspoken women from all walks of life who were joining the crusade, even going to prison for their efforts. Emily noted all this and felt her adrenalin rising. Where had she been all the time this was going on? Up in the northland helping to make a new life. Now that was done. The girls were grown, Arthur had his new interest: it was time for her to add her voice.

She began to raise political subjects at her parties and suggest group meetings to discuss the issues. She found herself sharing in problems for raising money for community projects. She got out to the outlying farm communities and talked to the women—women whose loneliness made them eager to welcome her—and she learned, as she sat sipping tea in their cosy kitchens, the injustices under which they lived.

Alberta had been one of the Territories before it became a province in 1904. A wife had no property rights in the Territories, one reason being so many men had married Indian squaws.

Under Alberta law at that time any man could sell his farm and walk off with the proceeds, leaving his wife and family to struggle on as best they could. Furthermore, he could will away his entire property, with no compensation for the role the wife had played in helping to build up its value. Nothing had been done to redeem the situation, nor was it likely to be done unless somebody started the ball rolling.

That is precisely what Emily Murphy did.

She marshalled her facts, she enlisted support from her friends, from the public, from organizations. She campaigned for the Dower Act—a law which would recognize a married woman's entitlement to a share of the common property in a marriage—wherever she went. She bored the family to distraction with it! She wrote articles about it and she studied legislative procedure, saying "She who would put on gloves must learn how to fight."

Emily found painting conducive to constructive thinking during the early years while Arthur was preaching in Ontario—though she produced nothing memorable, some of her oils are still around and enjoyed by members of the family. She found solace in another kind of painting, too. Whenever she was upset, angry or frustrated in her battles for social reform she took it out on the kitchen furniture. Arthur would often come home and find

Emily, sleeves rolled, paint-stained overalls buttoned around her ample middle, slapping a fresh coat of paint on a kitchen chair. Over the years, while she fought for this or the other reform, the kitchen decor took on a multicolored hue as she took out her frustrations with paintpot and brush.

Sometimes she despaired of ever having the Dower Act passed as the Bill was turned down several times. (One of the Members had snorted: "Why should a woman worry about a share in her husband's property while he's alive? Time enough after he's dead!")

But, for Emily, there were the distractions of a fast-paced life. There were hotel banquets costing fifteen dollars a plate to attend, to which women wore 150-dollar Paris gowns. Emily, who was no fashion plate, eschewed the Paris finery, preferring her own specially uncoordinated, flashily assembled collection of vivid colors, bows and ribbons. Some of the more snappish of her female friends showed open disapproval of her lack of style. "Look, there's Emily Murphy," they would whisper, "Isn't her hat ridiculous and old-fashioned!" Emily would hear, and the hurt would go deep,[3] but she would always bounce back, maybe to win a prize at the next fancy dress affair. (Attired as an early Saxon she won first prize at the Edmonton horse show on Major, some years later in 1919.)

During this time, and until 1912, Emily was Literary Editor of the *Winnipeg Telegram;* she was also putting the finishing touches to the manuscript of *Janey Canuck in the West,* which was published, and became an immediate success, in 1910. It is still in print today.

In moments of leisure the girls and Emily would shop for antiques which began to fill the house. Emily had become quite knowledgeable about old bibles while they were going from rectory to rectory in Ontario, and was the proud owner of a 1578 copy of the famous "Breeches" Bible, sometimes called "The Geneva Bible." It was one of her most prized possessions, along with some beautiful and treasured pieces of old crystal and china. Evelyn, the youngest daughter, inherited her mother's love of old things and became quite an authority on antique china and glassware in her later years, writing regular articles for various magazines on the subject.

In 1910, while still pushing for the enactment of the Dower Act, Emily found time to inaugurate a movement for the establishment of the Victorian Order of Nurses in the city, and another for the establishment of municipal hospitals in Alberta. In due course she became the first woman member of the Hospital Board of the City of Edmonton.[4] Public playgrounds were established due to Emily's perseverance. But the Dower Act was her consuming passion, so much so that when it was first turned down, the *Edmonton Journal* ran a piece which said: "Mrs. Murphy is so much in earnest over the Bill that its success is as good as accomplished. It may not be this year...nor the next...but this leader of women will keep hammering away until even the most obstinate man will be convinced that it is best to withdraw quietly and without further ado, let down the bars!"[5]

Finally, in 1911, the Dower Act was passed. It provided that a wife must get a third of her husband's estate, even when he did not leave a will. It was a significant achievement, a major victory for Emily—and her first. Congratulations poured in, but the first to rejoice with her in her hour of glory was Arthur. "I'm proud of you old girl," he said, holding her close and kissing her ear, "You've done it. All by yourself you've done it. If anyone deserved to win, you did. You showed 'em."

Emily smiled, but her eyes searched Arthur's face anxiously. "It's a good, good feeling," she said. "There are other things too, Arthur, will you..." she hesitated, "will you mind very much if I go on doing this sort of thing?"

Arthur shook his head. "What d'you say, girls?" he called to their daughters, now grown-up young ladies, who had rushed in to add their kisses and congratulations. "Shall we let our Tubbie loose to change the laws of the land?"

The girls flung themselves affectionately upon their mother, showering her with hugs and kisses. Evelyn, always the more demonstrative of the two, was shedding tears of happiness, and saying over and over again, "Oh, Tubbie, you did it, you did it."

When the uproar had died down a little, Arthur put in the last word. "We know the kitchen will be repainted this year," he said with a grin. "How about choosing the colour now, to save time?" He didn't even have to dodge the recipe book that Emily threw at him—her aim was always poor!

In the next few years Emily took on one responsibility after another. She paved the way for the election of women as school trustees in Alberta; she became vice-president of the Alberta Association for Prevention of Tuberculosis, and a member of the Charter Committee of the City of Edmonton; she became the Hon. Secretary for Canada of the Society of Women Journalists of England, holding the position for twelve years; and for seven years she was president of the Canadian Women's Press Club.

Her interests at this time were dominated by conditions in hospitals and one year she was asked to join the Ladies Committee on its examination of the local hospital. Little more than a gesture, this annual ritual always resulted in a pleasant, if somewhat vague, report which was duly filed. The ladies would arrive to find the staff in neat array, work progressing smoothly. The year that Emily participated, the inspection was a little different.

It started off with the usual expectations, but Mrs. Murphy startled everyone by straying from the carefully guarded group. She opened doors. She chatted to patients. She visited the kitchen. She poked, lifted, prodded, and sniffed. Her subsequent report was the sort that tended to straighten the hair of the ordinarily lethargic board: "Access to the fire escapes is blocked by beds, invalid chairs, and baby carriages." "Flushers for cleaning utensils are inadequate." "Nurses' quarters are poor." "Vegetables are not properly kept." "The nurses' dining room is next to the mortuary." (Comment unnecessary, noted Mrs. M.) The hospital, in her opinion, was overstaffed, yet the bills were not properly collected and the staff did not

C.W.P.C. Triennial Group at Paget Hall, Calgary.
Emily is in the front row, to the right of Colonel
George Ham

handle its work well. Added to which the hospital was running on a daily deficit of nearly a hundred dollars.

The report arrived like a thunderclap and was published under banner headlines by the *Edmonton Bulletin*. It was the subject of furious discussion at the next few board meetings, and there were some ungallant remarks made about "that Mrs. Murphy." There was, however, no rebuttal of the accusations.

During these years, Emily had two more books published, *Open Trails* in 1912, and *Seeds of Pine* in 1914. Both were collections of situation sketches adorned with her lively commentary. Rave reviews came in from major North American and British newspapers and magazines. *The Canadian News* (London), declared: "*Seeds of Pine* promises to go far beyond her other books as a surer, maturer, yet no less sprightly describer of virile life."

In *Open Trails* Emily describes a visit to Ottawa in which she shocked the Senate Chamber by appearing improperly dressed. It was the day the House opened, and she and Arthur were disappointed to find every available space in the Gallery occupied. As they were turning away resignedly, they ran into two friends, one a senator, the other a cabinet minister, who, learning of their plight, instantly took steps to rectify the situation. Up in the elevator, down the stairs, along passages "suggestive of intrigue and hair-breadth escapes," they were ushered, until finally a door opened and Emily gasped to find herself immediately in front of the Senate Chamber "with His Majestic Blackness of the Rod looking untellable things at me." The Cabinet Minister whispered to Black Rod, who replied impassively, "The lady is not in full dress," managing to invest the word "lady" with a degree of disdain calculated to frighten the most hardy female; it frightened Emily.

Thanks to the interventions of both senator and cabinet minister, however, Emily became the first woman attired in a street suit to take a seat on the floor of the Senate Chamber. She removed her hat and left it at the door, "where the Padre indecorously hid it under a bench," and was ushered with full pomp to her seat where she subsided among a sea of "splendidly groomed and plumed women."

In her first years in Edmonton, Emily travelled extensively, not only with Arthur, exploring, but on commission by magazines for articles and to conferences for the C.W.P.C. [Canadian Women's Press Club]. *Seeds of Pine* recounts some of these travels—and some of the escapades in which she became involved.

On one occasion Emily was sent to Grouard Landing, overlooking Buffalo Bay, by *Collier's Magazine* to do a series of articles on Bishop Grouard's Jubilee. She and several other writers travelled by steamer down the Athabasca River, across a portage of fourteen miles, and to another steamer which took them across Lesser Slave Lake to the northern shore and their destination.

Emily on the Athabaska

The trip took nearly five days. The boats were small and uncomfortable, and on the first night the purser informed Emily and her woman companion that there were sixteen bunks on the boat—and only eight mattresses. The purser hinted that a group of priests presently saying their prayers on the lower deck might be relieved of one or two of their mattresses...

The two women hightailed it to the priests' quarters with larceny in their souls. To give Emily her due, she did hesitate, feeling their plan to be "a plain and undeniable demonstration of wickedness..."—but her companion scoffed at such sentiments. When men took terrible vows not to get married it was women's stoutest duty to steal their mattresses whenever the opportunity served. "She also told me," said Emily, "some names which Clement of Alexandria, a Father of the Church, applied to women in the early days of the Christian era. She had read about it in history." Thus satisfied that their errand was justified, Emily overcame her principles and joined in the burglary. The following morning the holy fathers reacted to the theft, to which Emily confessed, with lively good humor.[6]

On the same trip Emily made a sentimental visit to the former home of her friend, the late Bishop Bompas, "The Bishop of the North," who became the subject of another of her books in 1929. "I finger the books in the library," she said, "with affection, in memory of the good Bishop who once told me kindly tales of these Indians who were his friends. And when I, too, have gone," she added, wistfully, "may it happen that some one who understands will touch my books in like manner, and say goodbye to them for me. I could not so endure it of myself..."[7]

On another fact-gathering trip Emily learned of The Helpless Affair, the ill-fated British Helpman Expedition to the Klondike ten years before, which culminated in the largest, wildest drunken spree the West had ever known. Emily sipped her lemonade in teetotal silence while she was entertained by some old-timers reminiscing over the last bottle of *Koch Fils 1892* left by the gentlemen adventurers...

On Christmas Eve 1896 the party, led by Lord Avonmore, arrived in Edmonton loaded down with superfluous equipment which was unusable, and supplies of gourmet food which were inedible. They had also brought brandy, liqueurs, champagne and wine in barrels, cases, kegs and demi-johns. Not being permitted to take this beyond Edmonton they decided to consume it, producing an orgy of drinking and fighting that continued unabated for six weeks.

Gradually Emily's travelling, which she loved so much, became restricted by her other responsibilities. She fought against it but knew it was no good. ("Why should I stay in town, I who only know the songs of the country? Why should anyone stay in a town which puts lines in her face; hardens her eyes; which spurs her feet and bridles her tongue?") There were important things to be done; it was as simple as that. *Seeds of Pine*, then, marked the end of her "songs of the country." It was dedicated to Emily's four brothers.

On June 27, 1911, Emily's mother died at the age of sixty-nine. Although the Murphys' enforced absences had separated Emily and her mother in recent years, they had remained close through correspondence and by as many visits as Emily could manage. The funeral was an opportunity for the rest of the family to be reunited for a brief time, and Emily had made the most of it. Tom had married, but Will and Harcourt were still bachelors, living together, and Annie had moved in with them. All three lawyers were successful King's Counsels; Will later became a Justice of the Supreme Court of Ontario. Gowan was a medical practitioner in the United States, where he now made his home.

Emily took advantage of the reunion to probe her brothers' legal expertise for answers to the many vexing procedural questions which now confronted her as she found herself appointed to various boards and spearheading movements to reform unacceptable legislation. Her ties with her three lawyer brothers, particularly, remained close to the end. Each one predeceased her: Tom was stricken with paralysis while pleading before the Supreme Court of Ontario in June 1923, aged fifty-eight, and never recovered; Harcourt, the youngest, died of a stroke in September 1927, aged forty-four, leaving over $153,000 in his will, a generous share of which Emily inherited; and Will, the Supreme Court Justice, died of a heart attack in November 1928, aged fifty-eight.

The Fergusons in 1911. Standing l-r: Thomas Roberts, William and Harcourt. Seated l-r: Emily, Gowan and Annie

Another major event took place in Emily's life in 1911, when Emmeline Pankhurst, the British suffragette, made the second of her stunning lecture tours on the North American continent. It was inevitable that she and Emily should meet, the fame of each having spread across their national borders. They became good friends from the first encounter, and Mrs. Pankhurst spent as many days and evenings at the Murphy house in Edmonton as her schedule allowed. They had, of course, much in common, and developed a profound respect for one another. Emily accompanied Mrs. Pankhurst on a tour of Southern Alberta in 1921, a trip to which she refers in an article in *Maclean's* magazine of that year. On another of her Canadian trips Emmeline taught Emily how to play solitaire, and made her a present of the small packs of cards she had used when in Holloway prison. The game fascinated Emily, and she quickly became addicted, finding it an excellent relaxation in the evenings after a busy day.

Mrs. Pankhurst gave several more lecture tours in North America over the following years. Soon after World War I, women having been given the vote, she was invited to Canada to lecture officially on public health questions. She stayed in Canada for several years, and had plans to settle there, but at sixty-five her health broke down and she was forced to return to England.[8]

Emmeline had led a stormy life since the turn of the century. A beautiful, but forceful woman, she had fought tremendously hard for the voting franchise for women, stirring crowds, raising money, and attracting legions of loyal and fanatical followers. One evening, at Emily's house, after the guests had gone, Emmeline described her release from Holloway (under the provisions of "The Cat and Mouse Bill")[9] which suggested the progress that women were beginning to make in their quest for solidarity. Emily includes it in her unpublished manuscript, *Emmeline Pankhurst in the North.*[10]

Three hundred of Emmeline's followers were informed that on a certain day and hour six weeks hence, she would carry a petition to the King at Buckingham Palace; they were invited to accompany her; they were also told the location of her hiding place, which actually looked out upon the palace itself. In spite of the astuteness of the Metropolitan Police, and of special detectives, and notwithstanding their freely offered bribes, not one woman uttered so much as a word concerning the matter. None of them told their husbands; none of them talked in their sleep; none of them got drunk. They were entirely taciturn. "Surely," notes Emily, "it was by no accident that the Romans deified Tacita, a woman, as the goddess of silence."

On the other hand, a slightly scandalized Emily remarked, "Emmeline Pankhurst is putting ungenteel and forward ideas in the heads of the women. They heckle the politicians," and she emphasized her opinion with a quote:

> If Queen Elizabeth had been alive today...
> said Mr. Lloyd George in a public meeting,
> "She would have been in Holloway," a woman shouted back.

With Emmeline Pankhurst

But Emily Murphy was undoubtedly impressed as she looked at the older woman who had suffered so much for what she believed in; impressed far beyond anything or anyone she had known before. Emmeline Pankhurst was also a most articulate and persuasive woman who would have seen in Emily the sort of material needed to extend the range of her cause, and bring the women of Canada into the fray.

An event of personal significance for Emily in 1912 was the publication of *Open Trails.* The event which was on everyone's lips in April of that year was the sinking on her maiden voyage of the White Star crack liner, *Titanic,* off the coast of Newfoundland, with the loss of 1,517 lives. It had been preceded by another tragedy in January of that year, when Robert F. Scott's expedition to the South Pole, fighting against terrible conditions, arrived to find they had been beaten by the Norwegian explorer Amundsen a month earlier. Crippled—and with the heart gone out of them—they had not survived the return journey.

These dark days were lightened somewhat when Earl Grey, then Canada's Governor-General, came to Edmonton to lay the cornerstone of Alberta's new Parliament Buildings. A ball was held in celebration—and Emily Murphy was in attendance. "In cream lace with red roses," she officiated at the introduction of that year's debutantes.

Then, in April of 1913, Emily travelled to Rochester, Minnesota, to the hospital of Dr. Mayo, to visit Annie who was a patient. While there, Emily became ill herself with cholecystitis, and had to undergo a major gall bladder operation. The Toronto *Globe* of April 15 listed Mrs. Murphy "In serious condition," and Arthur was sent for. Emily was scared, for there had been some fear it might be cancer. She describes in the reprinted edition of *Open Trails* how she passed the time after the operation: playing solitaire.[11]

The illness was the first indication of the diabetes which Emily had contracted. She was never heard to mention the disease by name, but it was a contributory factor in her death twenty years later. In 1913, little was known about diabetes; there was no cure, no remedy, and only the most elementary treatment was available. It would be 1922 before the first patients were treated with the newly discovered insulin. In the older person, diabetes may develop slowly; in the young it rampages through the body quickly and can be fatal within a year from diagnosis.[12] Emily was lucky in that she contracted it in middle age and its progress was slow. Her health was never the same, however, after the bout with cholecystitis, and her diabetes persisted, unchecked. The discovery of insulin might have come too late for her: when it did become available she never took it.

The Canadian Women's Press Club, of which Emily Murphy was president, was entertaining visiting dignitaries by the score. There were speeches to be made, committees to be organized, and a seemingly never-ending routine of teacups to be washed and put away. Even while she and her members hammered away at City Hall to do something about lowering the height of the streetcar steps, which at 16½ inches were too high for the elderly to manage without difficulty, Emily was watching with interest the career of another writer and outspoken proponent of women's rights: Nellie McClung.

McClung and her Political Equality League were making headlines in Winnipeg. Their most redoubtable opponent was the Premier of Manitoba himself, Sir Rodmond Roblin, who maintained:

> "Woman's place is in the home. Her duty is the development of the child character and the performance of wifely duties. To project her into the sphere of party politics would be to cause her to desert her true sphere, to the grave danger of society. Woman suffrage would be a retrograde step.... [You say] it has been beneficial over the line. But for every marriage in the United States there is a divorce..."

As a result of Premier Roblin's unyielding stand, the "Women's Parliament" was conceived by Nellie McClung and other P.E.L. members in a burlesque entitled *How the Vote was Not Won*, presented at the Walker Theatre in Winnipeg in January 1914. The audience filled the house to the rooftops, and were urged—men and women— to sign a suffrage petition to the government.

The play, which did more than anything else to break down prejudice against votes for women, reversed the real life situation and showed women legislators seated at desks in readiness for the first parliamentary session, addressing themselves to one absurd petition after another, concerning men. The play reached a crescendo when a deputation of men arrived with a wheelbarrow overflowing with petitions for votes for men. They were given short shrift on the grounds that if they were allowed to enter the political sphere they might neglect their proper business. Nellie McClung played the premier and based her portrayal upon her own interview with Premier Roblin. "Oh no," she exclaimed,

> "man is made for something higher and better than voting. Men were made to support families. What is home without a bank account? The man who pays the grocer rules the world. In this agricultural province, the man's place is the farm. Shall I call man away from the useful plough and harrow to talk loud on street corners about things which do not concern him? Politics unsettle men, and unsettled men means unsettled bills—broken furniture and broken vows—and divorce...When you ask for the vote you are asking me to break up peaceful, happy homes—to wreck innocent lives..."[13]

It brought the house down.

When Nellie McClung moved to Edmonton in 1914, Emily Murphy was one of her first callers. They hit it off immediately, and remained firm friends for the rest of Emily's life.

With war now raging in Europe there was an even greater sense of urgency for women's suffrage, and the Murphy-McClung team redoubled its efforts. Gradually their ranks swelled, apathy turned to interest, and Canadian women (and men) ceased regarding the issue as one of concern only to a few eccentrics given to chaining themselves to railings. In 1916, Alberta became the first of the provinces to grant women the vote.

By now, Emily was a Lady of Grace of the Order of St. John of Jerusalem, a decoration she had received in recognition of her writing and her social work.[14] She was a senior executive member of many national organizations, and had become deeply involved in working with women on various patriotic issues. Both she and Nellie grew particularly interested in a plan for registering women for voluntary war work and in industry, but despite being started the project was never completed.

A Federal appointment to the War Council of Women was responsible for Emily's much-publicized toiling in her wartime garden, nicknamed "The Rake's Progress," in an attempt to mobilize women to help increase food production. (As a gardener, Emily left much to be desired. She hated weeding, somehow never got the hang of planting, and always went into her garden with a book tucked in her blouse front.)

One of Emily's favorite aphorisms was: "Nothing ever happens by chance, everything is pushed from behind," and she must have had that saying uppermost in her mind on that Spring day in 1916 when, in response to the urging of the local Council of Women members, she visited the office of the Attorney General of Alberta, in an attempt to try and persuade him to set up women's police courts presided over by women, to try cases in which women were involved.

The result was that on June 19, 1916, Emily Murphy became the first woman police magistrate in the British Empire. Janey Canuck had come a long way, but would there be room for her under those magisterial robes? Some say no. Janey Canuck belonged to Emily's past, and there she remained when Magistrate Murphy took over. Yet many of Janey Canuck's endearing qualities lived on in Magistrate Murphy: humanity, compassion, a consuming interest in people and their problems, an ability to share their sorrows and their joys, joking and laughing with them. There were many times when some ludicrous situation would be unfolding in her courtroom, and Emily would have to change a chuckle quickly into a magisterial cough.

Group photo taken at McClung home in Edmonton. Centre: Nellie McClung, Emmeline Pankhurst, Emily Murphy. Mrs. McClung's son, Mark, is in the foreground

Chapter VII

The Black Candle: 1916-1926

How asps are hid beneath the flowers of bliss.

(from The Black Candle*)*

Despite an official request from the Attorney General's Department that Emily be given permanent quarters in which to conduct her hearings, civic authorities were slow, to say the least, in providing accommodation. As her cases piled up, Emily grew increasingly annoyed at the lack of cooperation. She made no secret of this, and the *Edmonton Bulletin* dated July 5, 1916 records:

> COURT ROOM REQUIRED. The Attorney General's Department writes to the Commissioners asking if Mrs. Murphy, the recently appointed magistrate for the Women's Court, may be provided with rooms in the Civic Block for the purpose of holding a court. The Commissioners have no vacant rooms in the block for this purpose, but will suggest that Mrs. Murphy use the Juvenile Court on the ground floor, which is now but seldom needed.

The Juvenile Court was acceptable to Emily, as a beginning, but if the Attorney General wanted her court in the Civic Block, then that is where she wanted it too. Notwithstanding her best efforts, however, it was not until six months later, on December 21, that the Mayor finally came to her rescue and confirmed that she was to have whatever rooms she needed on the sixth floor of the Civic Block for the Women's Court.

The lethargy with which civic authorities responded to the needs of the new magistrate starkly contrasted with the public and private acclaim which surrounded the appointment. From far and wide it came—telegrams, telephone calls, neighbors dropping in, strangers stopping her on the street: "Aren't you the Mrs. Murphy they've made a judge? ...A grand thing!" The British and Canadian Press carried the announcement the next day and other countries picked it up later. There were editorials, feature articles, and letters from all over the country, from friends, acquaintances, and people who knew her only through her books. However they said it, and the letters ranged from the unlettered to the eloquent, they all had the same theme: "It's a great thing they've done, to choose a woman at last."

Nevertheless Emily herself had misgivings. For one thing she knew nothing about law. "But you have three lawyer brothers," said Arthur, who was one of the new magistrate's staunchest supporters, when Emily confided in him one evening. "They surely will recommend books for you to read." They did, and Emily, with her usual thoroughness, ploughed through them all, memorizing the salient points of judicial procedure, with Arthur catechizing.

One of Emily's great strengths was her husband's total supportiveness. He made no secret of his love and the pride he took in her achievements. A man of abundant energy, he continued to pursue his own interests, develop his own friendships in business and sports, and the church still called upon him occasionally for some of his stirring sermons.

The Ferguson brothers were all enthusiastic about her appointment, and had been among the very first to send telegrams of congratulations (and advice). Harcourt wired:

LET ME OFFER MY CONGRATULATIONS TO YOUR WORSHIP STOP TRY TO TEMPER YOUR DECISIONS WITH MERCY AND DO NOT HAND OUT TOO MUCH OF YOUR OWN MEDICINE NAMELY HARD LABOUR STOP.

Eldest brother Tom, now a Winnipeg K.C., wrote:

Well done. In fact I say shake, Judge. The fact is that none of your brothers have yet been able to attain to a position on the bench, and as Fate had willed it that someone in the family must be a judge, you simply had to do it to save our face. Again, well done. You beat your brothers to it...While I am at it, Emily, be easy on 'them wimmin.' That is the one thing I am afraid of—that you may not possess sufficient gallantry to pass over many things.

And brother Bill had some words of wisdom: "Good morning Judge. Common sense and mercy are necessary attributes; legal knowledge a valuable qualification; pride, and sometimes a bad liver, are curses of most legal administrations."

In Bill's Osgoode Hall office a year or so later, Emily copied a letter from a well known poet-barrister, written on the occasion of her brother's elevation to the Bench:

I helped to make you a Bencher...Now let me speak from a safe position. You are the President of a wicked Tory club. You are evidently the member of a Church containing a large percentage of wicked men, and you know you are the friend and protector of the wicked. I, therefore, ask you not to forget your old friends when you come into your Kingdom. On the Bench be fair, but in cases of doubt lean somewhat to the wicked; they are grateful and human people and will appreciate your efforts.

> *With genuine congratulations, believe me,*
> *Yours truly,*
> *Jas. Haverson*

Emily framed her copy and kept it close by her desk as a constant reminder that, in her own words, "...even if people have committed an offence, and have been apprehended for the same, there does not seem to be any valid reason why they should be coarsely 'hustled' or dealt with unkindly."

Emily likened her first day in court to "As pleasant an experience as running a rapids without a guide." Everyone else, the lawyers and police officials, "looked so accustomed and so terribly sophisticated"—most of the time. In addressing her, many of them lost their calm efficiency and stumbled and stammered over "Your Worship" and "Your Honour," most calling her "Sir" and one prisoner even opting for "Your Majesty." The day saw a parade of prostitutes and petty criminals to be sentenced, but it also, in the second case of the day—a breach of the Liquor Act[1]—produced the first of several objections by a popular criminal lawyer, Eardley Jackson, to Emily's jurisdiction as a magistrate on the grounds that she was not a "person" within the meaning of the statutes. To her great credit, Emily refused to be intimidated, duly listening to and noting the objection, then proceeding with the hearing of the case. Her sense of humor was probably her greatest strength at this time, as she notes: "Other barristers caught up the objection and we had a merry time of it. He was a poor fellow indeed, who could not put up a new aspect of the argument..."

This sort of criticism continued for a few months, then died down—until the day when Alice Jamieson, Emily's counterpart in Calgary, had her status similarly challenged, with the result that the Alberta Supreme Court handed down the decision that women could not be disqualified from holding public office on account of their sex.

Emily was angered by the fact that the law had not been rescinded. While public opinion may have rendered it obsolete, technically it was still valid. She talked it over with Nellie McClung and others. For some time they had all been lobbying their Federal M.P.'s on the question of having women appointed to the Senate, but always with the same reply: The B.N.A. Act had made no provision for women, and the Members feared that women could not be appointed to the Senate until that great foundation of our liberties was amended, which would take time and careful thought. The clause in the Act dealing with the Senate appointments stipulated that "Properly qualified persons may from time to time be summoned to the Senate." To be "properly qualified," a person had to be a British citizen, at least thirty years of age, and possess four thousand dollars in real property. But always there was that stumbling block. Women might well be otherwise properly

*With Nellie McClung and Alice Jamieson in 1917,
on the day the Women's Suffrage bill was passed*

qualified, but were not *persons* under the Common Law of England.

Now the voices of organized women in Alberta were raised, demanding action on a national level. Emily tested the situation herself by allowing her name to go to the Prime Minister, Sir Robert Borden, as a candidate for the Senate. Her candidacy was rejected. As other Prime Ministers took office, other women presented their names, women's groups and clubs sent delegations requesting specific female appointments, but were also rejected on the same grounds: that women were not "persons." For ten years they persisted, only to be continually blocked on this simple technical point. There seemed no way around it, until brother Bill, the year before he died, drew Emily's attention to a provision in the Supreme Court Act allowing any group of five interested people to seek an interpretation on a constitutional point. That was all Emily needed.

The ten years between 1917 and the famous Persons Case of 1927 were busy ones for Emily on a more personal level too. Kathleen, now married to John Cleave Kenwood, had adopted a little girl, Emily Doris Cleave Kenwood, who became the apple of Emily's eye; a kind fate saw to it that she was spared the sadness of her granddaughter's suicide many years later, after her 1949 marriage to John Dundas Creighton in Vancouver.

Arthur had his own interests, too. He had gone into life insurance— according to the City Directory of the day—and was still called upon to preach from time to time. He enjoyed playing golf, an activity he kept up all his life (to the point where a reporter, wishing to interview Arthur for the local paper on his 90th birthday, had to wait until he had finished the last hole); he was also still very much the sportsman and outdoorsman.

It was inevitable that a new pattern would evolve in his and Emily's lives at this time, and there were people who wondered about this, and its possible effect upon the family. After all, they murmured, at sixty Arthur was still a virile, handsome man, and with Emily so busy with civic affairs, it would be no surprise, etc. etc.... But try as they would, they could never find a whiff of scandal surrounding the Murphys. Emily made certain that weekends, at least, were dedicated to family gatherings. Kathleen and her family were frequent visitors at Sunday lunch, when there would be bustlings and fun in the kitchen as everyone pitched in. Sometimes Emily's popular date and nut loaf would be presented at afternoon tea.[2] There is no reason to doubt that such occasions were unanimously treasured.

It is perhaps hard for us now to fully grasp how difficult Emily's magisterial role was in the beginning, how fraught with hazards at every step, as those who opposed the appointment waited for her to make her first mistake, show her first annoyance at the little humiliations she was subjected to (such as finding the court room booked to others when she had hearings), and other petty obstructionism. Strenuous objections on Emily's part would merely have lent credence to the claim that women were hard to work with, unreasonable and emotional over details. On the other hand, to have responded meekly to the cavalier attitude shown by many of the court officials to the appointment of a woman, would have quickly relegated her function to a secondary level and reduced her sphere of power to the ineffectual. Emily chose to meet these mean-spirited, under-cover attacks with firmness and with dignity. She faced the public with apparent serenity, stuck to her guns, and maintained her good humor.

Emily's ability to take a joke was never more in evidence than the day firemen at No. 1 Fire Hall obtained a woman's purse and put a corner of a twenty dollar bill near the clasp, making it look as though the rest of the bill was inside. They attached a wire to the purse, and when someone would stoop to pick it up, they would pull it away. Magistrate Murphy stooped— and saw the purse dart away. She may have been surprised, but she led the laughter that ensued, and the item made the columns of the local paper the next day.[3]

In turn, she loved to pull a gentle fast one on others. One morning, in the courthouse elevator, a nervous looking woman, the only other occupant, asked Emily on which floor was the Women's Court. Emily told her. "Are you concerned about a case?" she asked. The woman nodded. "Yes, I'm from the States to give evidence for a friend. I understand the Judge is a woman, and I don't like that idea one bit." "Cheer up," said Emily, lifting a red rose from her dress and pinning it on the woman's lapel. "Here, take this for good luck!" Minutes later, she made her dignified entrance to a standing court, and smiled to herself at the woman's astonished face.

It took time to win over the opposition to her appointment, but she did it. Officials, both male and female, who had looked forward to the failure of what they chose to regard as a novelty, lived to see the day when every man-jack in the department sang her praises, including the lawyer who had been the first to claim she had no right to sit in judgment. In fact, some years later, Emily was able to give this advice to new women magistrates: "You need not fret unduly about your ignorance of procedure. If you be studious and have a teachable spirit, you will find that the clerk of the court, the Crown prosecutors, the Deputy Attorney-General, his solicitors, the librarian at the Law Courts, and nearly all the barristers in the city, ready to help and advise. As a matter of fact, they will probably get to have a kind of paternal interest in your work and, on occasion, will even take abuse from you right in the courtroom. At least, they will if they are like the fine-fibred fellows of Alberta."[4]

Such is the price of fame that Emily's in-tray bulged with letters of thanks, pleas for mercy and intercedence on behalf of others, letters about bad conditions in jail, and letters from other magistrates remanding prisoners for Emily to deal with. There were letters addressed to "Mother Murphy" and "Dame Emily Murphy" asking for advice, making charges about neglected children; there were letters such as the one from a discharged prisoner thanking her for support of his character, and vowing "To show satisfaction by living a Godly, straightforward, honourable life." There were letters regarding domestic strife, incest, and from prisoners requesting parole.

There were chatty letters from prison addressed to "My dear friend Mrs. Murphy" and requesting commutation of sentence. There were official letters from the Attorney General's office, letters regarding drug problems, and letters from organizations such as the Dominion Prohibition Committee seeking her help for their "Strengthen Canada Movement." Correspondence flowed in from everywhere, and it was answered. In the evenings, after her day in court, Emily answered all these letters, sometimes typing or writing them herself; sometimes Evelyn would type them for her, after which they would have a snack and retire to bed. Even then, Emily was often disturbed later on by the doorbell and a police official requiring her signature on a search warrant.

Evelyn became very close to her mother during this time. She worked variously for the library, for the *Edmonton Journal,* and wrote articles on antiques for magazines and newspapers. She also did much of the housework and cooking and entertaining, though Emily usually employed household help—often girls who had come before her on a charge of one kind or another.

Emily's philosophy was that "A police court is a casualty clearing station. We magistrates should not be there to blister people but to help them." She was convinced that "The best way a woman magistrate, or any other woman, can be a saviour is not to stoop and save, but to stand by the girl and let her save herself."

A constant parade of girls who had fallen foul of the law were helped to save themselves in the household of Magistrate Murphy. Some people cast a jaundiced eye on these proceedings, but if Emily noticed, she remained unconcerned, and continued to employ whomever she chose. There is no indication that any of her erstwhile prisoners in the dock ever gave Emily any domestic trouble or proved a liability. On the contrary, they were often pathetically grateful.

Evelyn Murphy

Of all the trembling, hysterical, vicious, insane, arrogant, cruel and weeping souls who were brought before the magistrate's large, throne-like chair over the years, there were some who required special treatment. There was a vivacious old Frenchwoman, for instance, who told the court how she was playing the piano for a dance and to relieve her thirst drank plentifully of "the lemonade." In fact, she lost count of the number of drinks she took, until "*Ma foi!* those keys of the piano they stand up like teeth an' would not hold on a min'te." She ran home as hard as she could with "the teeth they follow after me like ten t'ousand crazy devils, till I have bad think in all my head." Then, she vowed, the police picked her up and brought her before Madame. It was abundantly clear to Emily that "no punishment or rehabilitation is needed in such a case."[5]

Then there were the two little girls who were left alone for some months on a bush homestead, forty miles from a railroad, and with no close neighbors. Their brother was overseas with the fighting forces, their mother was dead, and their father was serving a term in jail. Hearing of their plight, the city sent two probation officers to bring them in. There was no motor trail to the farm and the officers were obliged to walk a mile through the forest. Being strangers, they unintentionally scared the children, who led them a fine old dance around the trees for two hours before being captured.

"It took a long time," said Emily, "for me to establish relations in court, but, ultimately we came to a perfect understanding through my expressing a curiosity concerning their horses; whether or not these were 'single footers' and whether they balked on their front or their hind legs. You would never credit the freshet of talk that issued forth in the ten rapturous minutes following."[6]

Children were often called as witnesses in Women's Court, especially in cases of abuse. Nervous, sometimes quite terrified, they would approach the Bench timidly, expecting at the very least a most terrible dragon breathing fire to confront them. One summer day, seven-year-old Dorothy Sheppard stood on tiptoe to try and see over the witness box. "You must be lonely down there," said Emily, not looking or sounding at all like a dragon, "come and stand up here on the rostrum beside me. Do you understand what is meant by an oath?" Dorothy shook her head. "All right. Do you understand what Cross Your Heart means?" Dorothy shyly nodded, and the incident was fully recounted in the next day's *Bulletin* under the headline: TOT TAKES UNIQUE OATH. CROSSES HEART AND HOPES TO DIE.

"One of the most vexatious questions in the Woman's Court," said Emily, "is the fining of misdemeanants. If a girl be fined as a vagrant, or night walker, and pays the amount, the State virtually becomes a sharer in the traffic. Her fine becomes a licence fee until she is again apprehended, when another fine is paid....Moreover, this fee or fine is usually borrowed by her from the reprobate male persons with whom she is best acquainted, so that the girl-woman steps out of court with the entangling noose tied more tightly about her neck." The borrowed money, which frequently included counsel's fee as well as the cost of any appeal proceedings, sometimes ran into several hundred dollars. Emily did not see jail as the alternative, but rather a better adult probation system.[7] What these women needed was inexpensive legal counsel that would liberate them from the "pimps and white slavers." The "rascals" who currently charged anywhere from twenty-five to four hundred dollars to defend one of these women, were, according to Emily, "living on the avails of prostitution."

With some of the more experienced offenders, Emily showed just how tough she could be when the occasion warranted. She could spot a liar at thirty paces, and crocodile tears never moved her. She would listen quietly at first, then snap "Stop your lying!" and throw leniency out the window. But there was the other side of the coin too. Charges were rarely laid against women who had physically abused their husbands. One man, with both thumbs broken by having them pressed back, explained how the "Missus" was always trying to "mess me about." Another had a wicked gash over his eyebrow caused by a flying cup, and asked Emily to "Just send for Violet and scare her a bit."[8]

Threats upon Emily's life, in the form of anonymous letters and telephone calls, were common. They came from offenders disgruntled with their sentences. "There is one distinct benefit...to being a police magistrate in a woman's court," Emily wrote, "You will have the distinction...—albeit a graceless one—of having persecuted more perfectly pure, unoffending ladies than any other woman in your city."

In Women's Court, 1918

Emily Murphy's powerful sense of the dramatic was often expressed in court. On one occasion five unmarried mothers were before the Bench requesting that their babies be put out for adoption. Emily looked sternly from one to the other, then paused, and in a voice rumbling with portent told the dumbfounded group, "You have companionship in this crime, but your punishment will come when you see a group of children playing in the street...and you will wonder if one of them is yours."[9]

She was also very outspoken about the problem of securing convictions against women in "A Straight Talk on Courts," (*Maclean's*, October 1920):

...crimes by men are more frequently committed openly, while the woman's part is that of complicity. She instigates the crime, receives the goods after the man has stolen them, procures the girl for his immoral purposes, or carries the noxious drugs which he disposes of. It was probably an observer of this combination who gave expression to the odious dictum *'cherchez la femme.'*

Your sex has saved you, is a favourite expression of the latter-day magistrate, as though there were sex in sin or sex in soul, as though that soul, black for a man, could be shaded only grey for a woman.

Emily found it hard enough to deal with all this floating human wreckage, but she was completely unprepared for the extent of the illicit traffic in narcotic drugs, in which Canada at that time led the world; the ravages upon society that drug dependency was making was evident in her courtroom almost daily. She did not mince her words in castigating the men and women "who batten and fatten on the agony of the unfortunate drug addict—palmerworms and human caterpillars who should be trodden underfoot like the despicable grubs that they are."

She began to study the subject, helped considerably by her official position, which also brought her into active and intimate touch with the addicts and pedlars. Emily sought answers to some urgent questions: Who was responsible for the traffic? Could it be stopped and, if so, what methods should be adopted to that end? Her studies led to a series of articles in *Maclean's* which she later incorporated into a book.

Published in 1922, *The Black Candle* was the first book of its kind, and it has remained the most exhaustive study of the subject, still kept by government and public libraries. In it Emily describes the methods of drug-taking, the degeneration of the addict, trafficking, regional addiction patterns, the law governing abuse, international cartels, and more. She discourses upon them all—opium, heroin, cocaine, marijuana ("A new menace") and their derivatives, and leaves no doubt in the reader's mind as to the immensity of the problem in Canada at that time, for which she laid the blame squarely upon the influx of Chinese immigrants. In doing so, she completely reversed her previous stand that Chinese immigration should be encouraged; now she was faced daily with the human disasters which drug addiction produced. Indeed, she was so outspoken and even obdurate on the subject that, two years later, it called into question her capacity to judge a case involving a local doctor and the Chinese part-owner of a chop-suey restaurant, Mah Ling, accused of illegally trafficking in cocaine.

Magistrate Murphy's presumed bias (possibly impeding the due process of law), was the subject of keen speculation by the local press, at the time. However, in the Alberta Supreme Court ruling against the contention, Mr. Justice Ives commented: "I am biased against those who unlawfully deal in narcotics as I am biased against those found guilty of murder, but that is not enough to prevent a fair trial." Emily would already have had some sly amusement from the defence's added contention that, since the accused was a male, he was entitled to be tried before a male magistrate. This backfired when the same Mr. Justice Ives vowed he could see no evidence in the documents that the accused was a male, and overruled the objection.

On a May morning in 1924 Emily, with all eyes upon her, sat in judgment behind a large desk, her back to a window, in the R.C.M.P. barracks court. It was the first day of what had become known as The Hislop Case.[10] The case was a complicated one, involving a well-connected local physician, Dr. J. Hislop, suspected of dispensing narcotics illegally, an R.C.M.P. agent and one-time addict, the Chinese, Mah Ling and his partner, Mah Doon, numerous witnesses, and a spirited defence lawyer. In addition, the courtroom was filled to capacity with Chinese friends of the accused.

The trial lasted several days and was the subject of explanatory letters from Emily to her brother Will, who had asked to be kept informed of his sister's progress. One of her letters indicates quite clearly how much she had to rely upon the police and their greater knowledge of the law in certain instances; "That is the only consolation a P.M. has—the last word." She found the accused guilty, but imposed only the minimum fine and jail term, since he was to be deported anyway.

In *The Black Candle,* Emily describes how the trafficker, the unscrupulous physician and the druggist who asks no questions, operated:

> The peddling addict gets a prescription calling for an amount of morphine, cocaine or heroin to last him for quite a long time, but when he takes it to the druggist, only gets a portion of the drug called for. The druggist then gives the pedlar a box or bottle bearing the name of the doctor, the prescription number and other particulars. The box may then be filled time and time again from illicit supplies. Like the widow's cruse of oil, it never becomes quite empty. If the police find the pedlar with drugs in his possession, he has only to refer them to the covering prescription, in the face of which they are powerless to act.

Dedicated "To the members of the Rotary, Kiwanis and Gyro Clubs, and to the White Cross Associations who are rendering valiant service in impeding the spread of drug addiction," *The Black Candle* caused a profound stir nationwide among law enforcement and social welfare agencies, the medical profession, and a general public horrified beyond belief at what was going on in its own backyard. Gradually its impact began to be felt abroad, and the Secretariat of the League of Nations ordered many copies, one for each member of its committees interested in the traffic in narcotics. Provincial Departments of Justice urged their magistrates to impose more severe penalties. Statutes in some provinces were amended to include some of Emily's recommendations.[11]

A letter which Emily received from a young undercover agent working in England, is printed in *The Black Candle* in a chapter entitled "The Living Death." "His letter is of especial interest," she wrote, "as showing the mentality of a man who has been using narcotics for three years. Plainly, he has become super-sensitive and suspicious....A psychiatrist would probably declare him to be suffering from cocaine paranoia." An excerpt from the letter illustrates the aptness of Emily's remarks:

...of all agents of destruction, crime, degeneracy, and self-hypnosis, cocaine is pre-eminently the most potent, and...ordinary roads to hell do not even show on the same map. Cocaine is the unfairest gamester of all. It is the greatest deceiver any man ever applied to his senses. Whiskey is a true sport in comparison.

A man drinks whiskey and excites his passions. With most men its effect is purely physical as a stimulant, and while giving Dutch courage to his body, at the same moment it fogs his intellect.

Whiskey shows you plainly that if you enjoy the 'kick' today, you must suffer the misery tomorrow. You pay whiskey its due within twenty-four hours of its enjoyment. You know this beforehand, and may take it or leave it. If the 'kick' is worth the sickness, go to it.

But cocaine plays no such game. It never shows a fang, not even a pain, until it has you securely enmeshed. It would take more than your former will-power at its height to defeat it, for even if you do manage to abjure the actual drug, the memory and craving are ever present to torture you.

Cocaine takes all you hold dear in life today—love, honour, family, fortune, health—and in two weeks if you try to recall the awful trick it played you, you will find yourself justifying the cocaine. The only memories your mind retains are of those beautiful days of speeded intellect, super-intelligence, controlled passions and of the exquisitely clean mind, when you started using cocaine—those days when it was really bringing out all your better manhood; when its effect was like nothing on earth outside of ancient fairy tales; when your whole concentrated powers could not see any ill effect from its use but, on the other hand, an evident benefit to your whole existence.

Yes, it kidded you along, and you feel that so far as your case is concerned it has proven a blessing instead of a curse. Of course, you acknowledge to yourself that it might affect others quite differently but to you it was the real elixir of life.

Then, Mrs. Murphy, you wake up. There takes place a crisis in your life which, in weak intellects, usually results in an 'overdose' of something, the ambulance and, maybe the Potter's Field. However, if you are made of sterner stuff...you will then start a living death. You have the sense of hearing, but your mind is only conscious of a craving and of some memories. You look like a human being alright, but your fellows do not recognize you. Some sneer, some laugh, and some give you the sympathy that is *usually served out to the weakminded member of the family. In any and all cases you know you are being held in contempt...*

Few realized what Emily had gone through to assemble the material for the book, working with the police, abetting agents posing as addicts, seeing the physically and mentally wrecked users, even jeopardizing her personal safety as big league traffickers threatened to put an end to her militant anti-drug crusade. She defended the book from its few critics by saying, "*The Black Candle* deals with the moral, physical, mental, social, curative, legal, criminal, punitive, causative, historical, tragical, medical, financial, and even grimly humorous phases of the subject. There is absolutely no other book which does this."

To a friend she confided:

One of the compensations of the years is an increasing immunity to praise or blame. One gets too busy to bother. I have always felt it to be a sign of weakness to explain over-much. I did not write the book for money, fame, or dis-fame...The results I have had, have been eminently satisfactory...Do you know that this hard-headed old villain actually prayed that she would live to put over the story of the drug menace in Canada? (And a fool doctor told me I wouldn't.)...Having lived and accomplished it, nothing else matters. Only myself knows what I suffered in the whole undertaking, but that is past now, and the public have the story as they should have it.

Emily evidently felt so strongly about her exposé of this "unspeakable vice" in Canada that she entered herself (unsuccessfully!) as a nominee for the 1923 Nobel Prize.[12]

In 1921 there began between Emily and young, struggling writer, William Arthur Deacon, a relationship through correspondence which was remarkable in its candor, the range of its interests, and its spontaneity. The alliance developed into a warm friendship after they met, and continued through Deacon's marriage, fatherhood and literary successes and failures over the next twelve years, ending only upon Emily's death.

Its tenor at first was that of junior wordsmith delighted to receive a pat on the head from a highly respected, well-known and established writer: "...Tickled to hell," Deacon says in September of 1921. "[Your] flattery will get me a swelled head. You see, some of my young friends here think there's some distinction to my prose, but I never got it from a senior like you before!"

He reciprocated the praise in *National Life* in 1922: "There is more genuine adventure in Janey Canuck reading the Bible in bed on a wet morning, than most people get out of disobeying its injunctions." Deacon even managed to make a virtue of Emily's habit of gathering and quoting unusual bits of information gleaned from older writers. (She kept an exercise book in which she penned quotations she came across and liked, in no special order and unindexed.) "...Janey has a mind well-stored with the thoughts of master pen-men, which she uses with a skill alone sufficient to distinguish her work from the great mass of ephemeral productions."

As their friendship and their correspondence flourished, they talked freely of their respective problems, habits, activities, ideas and opinions on writing and publishing, with a frankness and sincerity that is as striking as it is a valuable source of information concerning two formidable writers who lived and worked at an important time in Canada's history.

From Emily's letters written between August 1922 and September 1933, many of them signed "Your old Bogey," we know that her health was breaking down. In a letter dated August, 1922 she commented: "It is a queer thing that I am alive and very vigorous, whereas he [the doctor] has died from the very ailment he diagnosed for me!" The ailment was, of course, diabetes. Over the next ten years there are frequent mentions of being "beastly ill," "Been ill, got thin," "Recuperating," "Not wasting away." Then, in a six page letter, she makes brief mention of being "In bed with that purely literary disorder known as 'a touch of jaundice.'" The letter was written September 7, 1933, just seven weeks before she died.

Letters were very important to Emily, not only the ones she received from the public but the ones she herself initiated. She was a compulsive letter writer, to family and friends of course, but also to others to congratulate, solicit, encourage, even to upbraid whenever it suited her purpose. She was forever working toward her goal: complete equality of opportunity for women and a better Canada for Canadians. To whatever post she was appointed—and they were many—she funnelled every scrap and every ounce of energy, imagination and drive. She fired off letters to prime ministers, governors-general, their wives, and leaders of the opposition, whenever their services, their names or their connections could be of help in her cause. Politicians, servicemen, industrial tycoons, the press—none were spared when she wanted action of one kind of another.

After the celebrated Persons Case had been won, she spotted an item in the newspaper concerning Rosa Ginsberg, first woman lawyer in Palestine, who was struggling to win the right to practise her profession. For seven years she had made one unsuccessful attempt after another to be called to the Bar. Emily wrote a letter congratulating her on her efforts, enclosing an account of the victorious Persons fight in Canada, and urging her not to give up. Weeks later, the Canadian papers carried an interview with Ms. Ginsberg in Jerusalem on her final success in which she paid tribute to the Mrs. Murphy in Canada for her words of encouragement; using the Canadian example in her arguments had helped her win the day.

When Emily noticed that Magistrate Hugh Macdonald of Winnipeg, seventy-seven-year-old son of Sir John A. Macdonald, had lost his leg in an accident, she sent him a sympathetic "What's a leg anyway?" type of letter to cheer him. It apparently did, for he replied that "The cheerful strain in which you wrote did me a lot of good...."

In 1919, the Murphys had moved to their final Edmonton home, 11011-88th Avenue, a charming house in their old neighborhood. Here, on a well-treed lot, amid comfortable furnishings, walls heavy with photographs of family and friends, they entertained a parade of visiting notables. At these times Emily would often display her collection of Indian relics, which she had dug up from time to time in Western Ontario, or perhaps her pieces of an old mosaic Roman road, given to her by one of the curators at the British Museum.

11011-88th Avenue, the house in Edmonton

The house was filled with interesting antiques and curios, but Emily spent most of her time in her own room where the walls were lined with books and her desk overflowed with papers. It was in this room that she grappled with the bulging shelves and drawers of papers and manuscripts, conducted her voluminous correspondence, noted down some legal point or other, or annotated her court cases. It was her inner sanctum, in which she recited poetry in the evenings "to get the taste of the court out of my mouth;" she set up her newly purchased "auto-phonic Victrola," and foxtrotted to it for fifteen minutes every night. "It is keeping me in sprinter's condition," she wrote to a friend, "when I run for the street car."

This, too, is probably where she experimented with smoking but decided she didn't like it.

Emily was unable to travel east to the funeral of her brother Thomas, who died on June 19, 1923, when he was only fifty-eight. When Arthur brought her the news the following morning, she sobbed for hours. When she was calmer, she wrote to William, Annie and Harcourt:

> *It had to come soon. A group of brothers and sisters that has held itself together for sixty years must prepare for inevitable dissolution. Yet now that the first rent has been made, I feel all the sadness of eternity in my heart. If there is any lesson to us, it means that the rest of us must line up closer than ever so that we may not, for a moment, lose the touch that binds.*
>
> *It is strange that he should have predicted, last Autumn, the very manner of his death. You remember we walked across the park from church, you and Annie ahead, and he and I behind. He said to me: 'I felt a wonderful happiness this morning that all four of us should have been in church and sat together.' Then he told me of his having such high blood pressure and that some day he expected it would likely 'take him' in court.*
>
> *...When he went over my manuscript for* The Black Candle *and wrote me his criticism and correction, I was amazed because of his judgment in literary matters, his keen sense of values. Personally, I know of no literateur in Canada who could have helped me as he did...We can only hope that each of us may find as serene an ending to our particular DAY and may leave a record as honourable and as exemplary.*

There were many messages of sympathy. One, a telegram datelined Ottawa, June 20, 1923, has been preserved among family papers:

PERMIT ME TO EXPRESS TO YOU MY VERY SINCERE SYMPATHY IN THE BEREAVEMENT YOU HAVE SUSTAINED IN THE LOSS OF YOUR BROTHER THOMAS ROBERTS FERGUSON KC

It is signed W L MACKENZIE KING

Some notoriety came Emily's way during the Ontario elections of 1926 in which government control of liquor in the province was the prime issue. The Prohibitionists endeavored to link her and the Ontario Premier, G. Howard Ferguson (who stood for control), as brother and sister, with vested interests in the distilling business. Emily was well known to be also for control in her home province. Both, of course, denied any such relationship, maintaining they were just good friends (which was true), but the newspapers had a field day and the furor did not die down until after the election. It was won handily by the premier, with not one Prohibitionist candidate elected.

Now another battle was shaping up, one which would not only change Emily's life but that of millions of women throughout the country. The battle lines for the Persons Case were being drawn, and Emily was to be in the thick of it. "Nothing ever happens by chance," she was fond of saying. "Everything is pushed from behind."

That is exactly the way it was.

Chapter VIII

Are Women Persons? 1927-1929

"The hand that rocks the cradle rules the world" is a prodigious untruth.
Women's sphere is still flattened at the poles.

When brother Bill uncovered the provision under Section 60 of the Supreme Court of Canada Act that any five interested persons had the right to petition the government for a ruling on a constitutional point, Emily reacted at once. She would invite four other women to join her in making that petition. After ten years of abortive unilateral measures resulting in a crying in the wilderness, what a relief it would be to have that battering ram in five pairs of hands!

She lost no time.

Nellie Mooney McClung, of course, was her first choice. She and Emily had become good friends and they agreed on most things; Nellie's comment when Emily asked her to be one of the petitioners ("I think the five of us can be depended upon to set the furze afire...") was one Emily herself could have made. Now living in Calgary, Nellie was an indefatigable worker for women's rights, and a staunch supporter of Suffrage and Temperance. Soon after the McClungs' arrival in Edmonton she had been elected to the Alberta Legislature where she was a Member for five years, until defeated on the prohibition issue in 1926. Schoolteacher, homemaker, author, crusader and politician, she would be a tower of strength to their undertaking.

Louise Crummy McKinney. A determined battler (some said a fanatic) in her crusade against the evils of alcohol and cigarettes. However, her deep involvement in public service (she was the first woman in the British Empire to take her seat in a Legislative Assembly), did not limit her to these two issues, and she identified closely with other feminist objectives. Born in Ontario, sixth in a family of ten, she moved to Alberta in 1903, a few years after her marriage.

Henrietta Muir Edwards. A tiny woman, with flashing brown eyes, Montreal-born Henrietta Muir had always been interested in the plight of others. At the request of the Canadian Government in 1908, she compiled a summary of Canadian laws pertaining to women and children. Her interest in law stayed with her and resulted in two books: *The Legal Status* of Women in Alberta and *The Legal Status of Women in Canada.* A vigorous campaigner for women's rights, her knowledge of the law was of inestimable value in the Persons Case.

Irene Marryat Parlby. English-born, raised in India (where her father was a Colonel in the Imperial Army Engineers), schooled in Germany, Irene Marryat met and married Walter Parlby in 1897, and settled on a ranch near Alix, Alberta. She immediately became president of the Alix local of the United Farm Women of Alberta, and later the provincial president of the organization. In that capacity she was elected to the Alberta Legislature, was appointed Minister without Portfolio and held the position for fourteen years. She placed a high emphasis on education, and in 1924 returned from a fact-finding mission to Europe armed with ideas for improving Alberta's educational system. Irene Parlby was a graceful woman with impeccable manners and style, but without affectation.

Nellie McClung

Louise McKinney

All the women accepted Emily's invitation, and so one day near the end of August in 1927, they gathered at Emily's home on 88th Street in Edmonton. It was a perfect early fall day, hazy, with the smell of hay in the air. Bees droned in the delphiniums and roses. The five women sat on the verandah talking the afternoon away, to the accompaniment of endless cups of tea and slices of date and nut loaf. They swapped stories. All of them were well-travelled speakers, each with a fund of anecdotes from her experiences. The irrepressible McClung entertained the little group with her favorite story about the time she bought an Accident Insurance Policy for five thousand dollars at a railway wicket before leaving on a lecture tour.

The cost was $2.50 for ten days. Casting her eye over the policy she noticed all the clauses which mentioned payments for disabilities began: "If the insured be a male..." On the back of the form it stated: "Females are insured against death only."[1]

Henrietta Muir Edwards

Emily had a couple of stories of her own. One time she was addressing a meeting in Toronto and the Mayor, who had dashed in a little late and out of breath, introduced her as "Sylvia Pankhurst." And then there was the time Premier John Oliver of B.C., upon being introduced as her dinner partner at an inaugural meeting of the Canadian Authors' Association in Edmonton, squeezed her hand so vigorously three times that it burst open her little finger, already injured when Emily had fallen down the stairs at the police station in high heeled slippers, on one of her nocturnal visits.

There were probably many other tea parties going on in Edmonton that lazy late summer afternoon, but not another like this one. These were not society's conventional "ladies," indulging in idle small talk, little fingers delicately poised above the handles of their cups. These women were movers and shakers, women with the spirit and the spunk to speak up on subjects they believed in, caring little what enemies they made along the way, but caring dearly about the converts they drew to their cause.

Irene Parlby

Now they had an objective which, if successful, would ensure that in future women would have the right to assume public office without equivocation and without censure. This fight would take them to the highest judicial court in the English speaking world, and take two years of undivided and concentrated effort before it was brought to a successful conclusion. Undeterred by the awesome obstacles they knew were ahead, they discussed the business at hand, and agreed there were three clauses of the B.N.A. Act of 1867 which merited closer scrutiny:

Section 21, describing the makeup of the Senate, contained nothing to bar females. Section 23, describing the Qualifications of a Senator, used only the masculine pronoun "He." The cause of all the trouble, and the clause to which various counsel had alluded when they objected to women acting as though they were Persons, was Section 24:

The Governor General shall from Time to Time, in the Queen's Name, by instrument under the Great Seal of Canada, summon qualified Persons to the Senate; and subject to the Provisions of this Act, every Person so summoned shall become and be a Member of the Senate and a Senator.[2]

The petition to which the women gathered on Emily's porch that August day in 1927 appended their signatures was simply: Does the word Persons in Section 24 of the B.N.A. Act of 1867 include female persons?

There were other questions to be asked too, and Emily lost no time in getting them answered. Yes, said the Department of Justice, the question submitted was considered to be of sufficient national importance to be presented to the Supreme Court; and yes, the five appellants could name their own lawyer; and yes again, the Department of Justice would pay all "reasonable fees" arising from the case on their behalf.

Emily attached a covering letter to the petition; at her insistence, the five appellants were listed in alphabetical order, so that the document, and any reference to it thereafter, was always in the name of Henrietta Muir Edwards. Emily may have come to regret her unselfish gesture later, for, although each of the others was emphatic about giving credit for the whole idea to Emily, there were some occasions afterwards when Henrietta (much to Emily's disgust) did nothing to dispel the natural assumption that since her name headed the petition she was the principal challenger.

The women appointed the Hon. Newton Wesley Rowell, K.C., a known supporter of female suffrage, as their counsel; it was he who argued their case before the Supreme Court of Canada in March 1928. It was April 24 of that year before the Supreme Court made its decision known. It had found for the Crown: women were not to be regarded as persons. In arriving at the decision, the Supreme Court justices had accepted the argument that the B.N.A. Act must be interpreted in the context of the time in which it was passed; since women held no public office of any kind in 1867, *ipso facto* the Founding Fathers could have had no reason to invite women to sit in the Senate.

Counsellor Rowell, on the other hand, had cited one instance where when the masculine gender was used, it was interpreted to refer also to the female, and another where in 1920, the word "persons" in Section 41 of the B.N.A. Act had been interpreted to include females.[3] But their combined worships had not been swayed, and their decision came as a stunning blow to "The Alberta Five" as they had become known. Nellie McClung takes up the story:

> We met again, this time in Calgary, and contemplated our defeat. Mrs. Murphy was still undaunted. We would appeal the Supreme Court decision. We would send our petition to the Privy Council [in London].
>
> We asked her what we would use for money. Lawyers' fees we knew were staggering. When a lawyer is writing his fee for a service of this kind his hand often slips.
>
> Mrs. Murphy said she would write to the Prime Minister. Perhaps he could devise a way. This was every woman's concern, and she was sure that the government would be glad to have it settled. The letter was written and we had a prompt reply. Newton Wesley Rowell was going before the Privy Council in October and had generously agreed to take our petition.[4]

There were a series of postponements and delays as a persistent Emily questioned the Deputy Minister of Justice in Ottawa:

January 4, 1929

With uncomplaining patience—I think I may even say with excellent grace—we have already borne three or four perturbing delays...

We are [now] instructed that the hearing of our Appeal is still further postponed, this time until April 29, and again because of something in connection with [a] wholly unrelated problem...

A reply from the Deputy Minister on January 12, 1929 was unrepentant: "*I am not aware of any interests of the petitioners which will suffer by reason of this appeal being deferred for hearing until the summer sittings...*"

There was nothing to do but wait.

Emily had barely recovered from the shock and sorrow of the untimely death at forty-four of her youngest brother, Harcourt, in September of 1927, when beloved brother Will, after a lengthy illness, passed away a little over a year later; since then she had immersed herself in her writing, in what spare time her court duties left her, and had become involved with various social causes.

A long-standing interest in mental hygiene had resulted some years before in Emily's organizing the first branches of the Canadian Committee of Mental Hygiene in Saskatchewan and Alberta, and becoming a member of the national board of directors from 1918 to 1925. Because of her facility with a pen she was always in demand for fund-raising; her pen was also eloquent on the need for more openness on sex, birth control, family planning, venereal disease and juvenile delinquency. In 1928 she openly advocated the distribution to all over sixteen of films such as *The End of the Road,* produced by the Canadian Social Hygiene Council, which dealt candidly with those topics. "If any think that ignorance is bliss or even a virtue," she said, "they should see this [film]. The story is told with restraint and delicacy but with power."

As a member of a citizens' committee looking into conditions in Alberta's asylums and jails, Emily had reported to the Alberta Women's Institutes that, although their province had a fine record, the situation was deteriorating rapidly. Accommodation was woefully inadequate, and could cope with only 1,700 of the more than 30,000 needing care, and costs province-wide had ballooned to 7.5 million dollars annually. Because of the uncontrolled influx of immigrants, who accounted for seventy percent of inmates, and the practice of releasing less serious cases from overcrowded institutions to make room for the dangerously impaired, an already desperate situation was escalating. Released inmates were fathering mentally handicapped children who, in time, would be likely themselves to require institutional care. Wives of inmates being released pleaded with Emily to recommend sterilization of their husbands beforehand or, "I'll have the operation myself, Mrs. Murphy," threatened one.

Consequently, Emily was a staunch advocate of sterilization,[5] a direct result of her close contact with the crimes, family breakups and unwanted pregnancies resulting from the release of all but the most dangerous of inmates from the mental institutions of the day. Those who concerned themselves with the issues were agreed that it was a matter of urgency to do everything possible to prevent the situation from getting out of hand, but, sensitive issue that it was, few were willing to move very far on it without the approval of the electorate. This is why writers like Emily Murphy were trying to bring the facts before the people, on the basis that a public danger needed a public warning. "I know of no way of driving a nail other than by hammering it," said Emily. And that is precisely what she was doing. It seemed the only way, then.

She also had firm beliefs on capital punishment, maintaining that prevention and not retaliation was to be preferred. "It is better," she was often heard to say, "that a youth convicted of murdering a father with five children be put to work for life, his wages going to aid the victim's family, than to be given the death penalty."

Emily had started writing the manuscript for a book called *Pruning the Family Tree* which stressed the need for family planning and birth control. In a letter to her friend Bill Deacon, she said, "I won't have any friends when it comes out as I'm saying a lot of things about the hierarchy, and about the inconsistency of the Church...Oh yes, all the truths I've wanted to tell for years..." The controversial manuscript never did find a publisher willing to risk his neck to print it.

Trial marriage was another topic much in the news. In "Companionate Marriage" (*Chatelaine*, May 1928) Emily gave it short shrift:

> The chief concern of society is with nesters and birdlings. Any system that interferes with this should be promptly stepped upon by a heavy and well shod shoe, rotary pressure to make sure. If civilization is to endure, we must preserve marriage. For all time it must remain a matter of public concern and not solely an arrangement between the parties thereto.
>
> There was once a man in Winnipeg who objected to certain culinary tasks in the kitchen and who, accordingly, quoted scripture to his wife, aiming to show that these, with the task of dishwashing, had been properly assigned to women. It was from the 2nd Book of Kings, Chapter 21, and Verse 13 that the woman made answer to him: *I will wipe out Jerusalem as a man wipeth a dish, wiping it and turning it upside down.* The Winnipeg man is still doing the dishes.

(Emily smiled to herself as she wrote those lines, recalling Arthur's frequent comment: "My dear old girl, you only know just enough scripture to be troublesome.")

She ended this reflective piece with advice for the newly enfranchised twenties' flapper: "In the marriage relation, as in the world of affairs, the question of who shall rule is one which must be worked out by the individuals...Whoever obeys a force commands it. Although love neither gives nor takes receipt in full, the secret of demonstration, for the most part, lies in non-resistance. This is a wonderfully fascinating exercise and one that either a husband or wife may depend upon to yield immense returns in happiness and richness of life."

Emily Murphy's own marriage was a striking example of this philosophy.

Women's emancipation had ushered in a new social climate in which it was confidently believed a woman now would have the same sexual freedom as a man in a marriage of equal partnership. Magazines and newspapers filled their columns with opinions pro and con, and "Janey Canuck" joined the fray. In 1927 Emily wrote "Obedience in Marriage" for the *Canadian Home Journal,* an amusing, lighthearted and discerning piece. Maintaining that the word "obey" in the marriage service was a sad survival of Saxon England "when a bride was transferred like a piece of land, and when part of the wedding ceremony consisted of touching her head with a slipper," she thoughtfully posed both sides of the issue: "Husbands do not promise to obey their wives, but the average man does ...Some persons naturally rule, others naturally obey. In the end, the fittest survive."

Emily was still very active in the Canadian Women's Press Club, although she had relinquished her post as president some years before, and had taken on the less visible role of historian. Since becoming a magistrate she had been keenly interested in conditions in Canadian jails, visiting them, talking to the inmates (some of whom she herself had sentenced), writing and talking about them and generally moving heaven and earth to take action if they did not come up to scratch.

How, Emily often wondered, did Canadian jails compare with their American counterparts? When she learned that her friend and C.W.P.C. colleague, reporter Lotta Dempsey, would be visiting the United States on a story, it seemed obvious to Emily that Lotta might, on some pretext or other, arrange to get herself thrown in an American jail and report her findings upon return. She was most persuasive and young Lotta, whose admiration for Emily knew few bounds, was quite game. Neither of them, however, had reckoned on Lotta's father, who vigorously nipped the project in the bud.

For Dominion Day 1927, Canada's Jubilee Year, Emily wrote "Confederation and the Destiny of Canada" for the *Western Home Monthly*. In it she posed these questions: "How can we love a country that is so big—cradled by three oceans—that it is more a continent than a country? Where from sea to sea...alien races have trekked their way across the land in long and lustful lines, each anxious for advantage to his particular 'ist' or 'ite'...? What cares the Scandinavian of Alberta or B.C. for the little provinces of Eastern Canada where there is not a mountain worth mentioning?" Her answer was a stirring call to patriotism:

> We are nine provinces in Canada...and this is our Jubilee...Confederation...the day we tied together all the little settlements of a big land and called them Canada. There are disconsolate people who say that because of the disabilities the West has been obliged to suffer, that, accordingly, we should secede from Confederation. It is a poor line of talk...Our patriotism cannot and does not rest on anything as variable as freight rates. Canada is not statistics. Canada is not a map, not a government. A great nation cannot be made, cannot be discovered and then coldly laid together like the pieces in a picture puzzle. No! Canada is a theme; it is a tune, and it must be sung together; or if you will have it so, Canada is a coat of many colours, but it is a seamless garment.

While one important Canadian achievement was in the making in 1927, two significant ones took place on the world scene that year, both of which heralded giant steps in the march of progress. On May 20, Charles Lindbergh's "Spirit of St. Louis" lifted off from New York's Roosevelt Field for Paris, landing 33½ hours later and establishing for the young pilot a firm place in world aviation history—and instant fame on two continents. The other was a movie, starring Al Jolson and 291 spoken words, which heralded, on October 6, the birth of talking films.

With the Persons Case still hanging fire, Emily decided she needed a holiday; although it was "Too early for dog races, too late for horse races," she and Evelyn visited Mexico for a few weeks. It was, I think, indicative of the strain that Emily was under that she distanced herself from her usual holiday haunts, knowing that she needed to restore her strength and vigor for the coming battle with the Privy Council. Upon her return, and to keep her mind occupied, she picked up the threads of the manuscript for a small book she was writing, principally for schools, about an old, departed friend.

Right from the start *Bishop Bompas* piques our interest:

When William Carpenter Bompas, a young Anglican clergyman from Regent's Park, London, went as a missionary in 1868 into the great polar desolation known as the Arctic Circle, the Eskimos took him for a descendant of Cain.

According to their legends, there were two brothers in the first family of mankind and one killed the other, the murderer afterwards disappearing into the frigid parts of the world. How many years ago this was they could not calculate, but, at any rate, it was quite evident that the young man, who had now come into their more pleasant region, was the son of Cain. This does not seem to have caused any hostility toward him, for, in writing of these people later, Bompas said that in all the world there was nothing warmer than the grasp of an Eskimo's hand....

Bompas spent forty years in the North, coming out only twice. On the first occasion, he went to England to be elevated to the episcopate. The second was shortly before his death.

Taking into consideration his loneliness, as well as his hardships and sufferings, the statement made by one of his associates, that he was the most self-sacrificing bishop in the world, is probably correct. Be this as it may, no name looms larger in the missionary annals of our Canadian North.

After chronicling the arduous journeying and good works this self-described "detached cruiser" accomplished in the many years he devoted to his beloved Arctic, Emily concluded:

Whether or not Bishop Bompas adopted a program, as one follows his labours in the northern hinterlands of Canada, and sees him working as translator, writer, teacher, doctor, voyageur, geologist or administrator, it gradually dawns upon the mind that 'the romance of the North' is a term often used but seldom understood. [It] is not properly applicable to the country itself, but to peerless men like William Carpenter Bompas, who have been romantic in spite of their setting.

Emily came down with a severe case of influenza early that year. The family worried when she took to her bed like a docile lamb; usually it took the equivalent of an armed guard to keep her under the sheets.

One Sunday evening the telephone rang. Assuming it was another of the many well-wishers who had been calling all week, Evelyn answered it and was surprised to hear sounds of music from the other end. The caller introduced himself as George Gregson of the travelling British Beggars Opera Company. He wondered if the lady judge was asleep yet? No, Evelyn said.

"Does she have a telephone handy?"

"On her bedside table."

"Has she any objection to secular music on Sunday at ten by the clock?"

"None whatever."

With Evelyn holding the telephone to her ear, a delighted but barely conscious Emily enjoyed the strains of "Come to the Fair," sung by members of the travelling Beggars Opera Company from Britain, with Zaidee White, the great soprano, at the piano—which she also did superbly well. On tour in Edmonton, the troupe simply had not been able to resist contacting their favorite judge.[6]

By the spring of 1929, aware that the Persons Case would be decided before the year was out, Emily kept as busy as she could. Besides court, there were the kitchen windows in need of repainting—and Arthur was preaching quite often again and surely could use her help...

"Have you finished your sermon for next Sunday yet, Arthur?" she queried one evening.

"M-m-m, almost," came the reply from the depths of the chair, over the top of which she could just see his head.

"Want any help? I could type it for you if you like."

"No thanks, old girl. Evelyn will do that, and I'm almost finished. You at a loose end?"

"Not at all." She fidgeted. Damn men. "I've got plenty of my own work to do." She stomped out to the kitchen. Kathleen and the family were coming over on Sunday. She'd bake a date and nut loaf, or a pie, or something. The hearing was July 22—would she ever live so long!

Hearing her mother banging about in the kitchen, Evelyn came down to help. "Mother! What on earth have you been up to?" she exclaimed from the pantry where she had gone to get some flour. "Look at all this stuff! It'll be months before we can use it all up." Bushels of potatoes, bags of flour, sugar and raisins, and jars of jams (including gooseberry) were stacked in a corner and on the shelves.

Emily was worried; her siege mentality had taken over again. Of course she denied it, insisting that the food had been an absolute bargain; she refused to admit for an instant that she had given in, once again, to her penchant for stockpiling in times of stress. Evelyn knew better than to argue, and the two of them clattered around the kitchen, while Arthur, putting the finishing touches to next Sunday's sermon, smiled to himself. Dear old Em. He hoped this thing went through for her—no telling what would happen if it didn't; he grimaced at the thought and went for a turn in the garden.

Emily spent her summer holiday that year in the back garden, "under a vividly coloured Palm Beach umbrella, surrounded by the tallest of tall sunflowers." These sunflowers were the offspring of those which her mother had brought from the garden of her father, Ogle Gowan, sixty years before, and planted in her Cookstown garden right after she was married. Emily was inordinately proud of those sunflowers and their heritage.

As the day of the hearing drew closer, Emily pondered more and more the possibility that the judgment might not go in their favor. While the Attorney-General for Alberta was supporting the appellants, the Dominion of Canada was upholding the Supreme Court's negative decision. It could go either way. She wrote to Attorney Rowell just before he left for England to argue the case on their behalf, and to put forward a contingency plan should the decision go against them:

> *I note that the Prime Minister goes to England presently, to a conference on Imperial Affairs. As his government, through the Minister of Justice, has promised to 'devise means' whereby women may serve in the Senate, it has occurred to me that in the event of our Appeal not being successful, the aforementioned 'means' might be devised at this conference—that is to say, the Canadian status might be made entirely clear in this, and in other matters, generally.*

That was Emily, leaving no stone unturned.

The hearing was held in London on July 22. Lukin Johnston of the *Canadian Press* wrote this eyewitness account:

> In a quiet room at Number One, Downing Street, five great judges, with the Lord Chancellor of England at their head, and a battery of bewigged lawyers from Canada and from England, are wrestling with a question, propounded on behalf of their sex, by five Alberta women.
>
> The roar of London penetrates only as a distant murmur. Room thirty feet high. Walls lined with shelves filled with leather-backed volumes. Judges sit at a semi-circular table. They wear no robes, no wigs. Just ordinary, everyday business suits.

Lord Chancellor Sankey, grim of countenance, and of few words, sits in the middle. On his right is Lord Darling whose eyes twinkle and whose lips twitch, as every now and again he cracks an irrepressive [sic] joke. Next to him is Lord Tomlin. On the Lord Chancellor's left is Lord Merrivale, famous as President of the Divorce Court, and next him, is Sir Lancelot Sanderson.

On the table before them, are voluminous documents, and legal papers, brought to them ever and anon by watchful attendants. Each of them has a glass of cold water beside him. The only ornaments on the table are three large silver ink-stands. In front of them, below the low barrier, are arrayed the counsel, in wigs and gowns...Rowell stands at the little rostrum in the middle, and propounds his arguments. A few members of the public, including half a dozen women, two or three bored-looking reporters, and a couple of ushers, make up most of those present.

It is all very orderly and dignified. Everyone is very polite. Mr. Rowell makes a statement, or reads long extracts from the B.N.A. Act. Lord Merrivale, ponderous and very wise-looking, asks a question, and Mr. Rowell replies in many words.

Deep and intricate questions of constitutional law are debated back and forth. The exact shade of meaning to be placed on certain words is argued to the finest point.

And so it goes on, and probably will continue to go on for several days. At the end of all these endless speeches, lessons on Canadian history, and questions by five great judges of England, it will be decided, if one may hazard a guess, that women undoubtedly are Persons. Which one may say, without exaggeration, most of us know already!

Judgment was reserved. It took the Privy Council three months to resolve their findings, but on Friday, October 18, 1929, Lord Sankey delivered the verdict which reversed the Canadian Supreme Court decision: Women were Persons and were therefore qualified to become members of the Senate in Canada. Part of their lordships' statement reads: "The exclusion of women from all public offices is a relic of days more barbarous than ours...and to those who ask why the word [person] should include females, the obvious answer is, why should it not?...Their lordships have come to the conclusion that the word persons includes members of the male and female sex, and that therefore the question propounded by the Governor-General must be answered in the affirmative; and that women are eligible to be summoned and become members of the Senate of Canada."

It is interesting to note the differences in interpretations of the Supreme Court of Canada and the Privy Council in London. The Supreme Court decided unamimously in their decision that women were forbidden to become Senators unless they were specifically mentioned to be eligible.

Lord Chancellor Sankey arriving with the verdict

The Privy Council took the opposite view: unless women were specifically prohibited from being in the Senate they were eligible.[7]

The Five were understandably jubilant. Emily hugged Arthur, and was hugged in turn by Evelyn, Kathleen, Cleave and little Emily Doris Kenwood. The other women heralded her as the force behind the petition. The landmark decision would have far reaching implications, and the press had a field day with it. History had been made. Congratulations poured in, and speculations were rife as to who the first woman Senator would and should be. Emily tried to inject some order into the chaos:

> "It should be made clear that we, and the women of Canada whom we had the high honour to represent, are not considering the pronouncement of the Privy Council as standing for a sex victory, but, rather, as one which will now permit our saying 'we' instead of 'you' in affairs of State."

The day after the Privy Council's decision, the *Edmonton Journal* printed the banner headline: MAGISTRATE MURPHY DESERVES ALL CREDIT MRS. McCLUNG SAYS. From her home in Calgary, Nellie issued this statement:

"We are naturally elated, though I must say we never despaired of ultimate victory. I am particularly glad for Mrs. Murphy's sake. It was she who discovered that any five subjects could ask their government for an interpretation of any point of law, and she saw in this a way of forcing the question of women's eligibility for the Senate into the arena of discussion. It was she who wrote all the letters, and arranged every detail in the controversy, assuming all the expense and labour involved. Her handling of the whole matter has been a masterpiece of diplomacy and to her the victory belongs."

Henrietta Edwards was also characteristically forthright: "This decision marks the abolition of sex in politics. Personally, I do not care whether or not women ever sit in the Senate, but we fought for the privilege for them to do so."

There were parties, luncheons, gala suppers, and every other kind of function organized by women's groups in honor of The Five, most of which they had to decline from sheer inability to be in three places at once.

Emily, Nellie and Irene Parlby were at the Macdonald Hotel in Edmonton one night having a little get-together in Mrs. Parlby's suite. "As they came down in the elevator and out into the rotunda," reported one of the little magazines, "they were laughing and talking like a group of teenagers. Mrs. Murphy did not giggle," the report went on, "she laughed—and so did the other Irish woman Nellie McClung. Next day it was all over town that three women came rolling out of the Macdonald drunk as lords which, of course, was funny to those who knew they were all teetotallers."

Emily received dozens of congratulatory letters; there was one from The Six Point Group in London, England, an organization heavily laden with aristocratic names on its masthead:

Dear Judge Murphy,

It is with the utmost pleasure that I take this opportunity of writing to you...Your victory was a deserved one, your action will influence the whole world to raise the status of women. As we go on our way towards the elimination of all discriminations based only on sex,...the way is cleared and smoothed by each such victory as yours....

We here in Britain are peculiarly [sic] *heartened just at the moment when we are planning the action to be taken to enable women to enter the House of Lords. Your winning of the right to enter the Canadian Senate cannot but weaken the opposition to the right to enter the House of Lords. We take courage from your action and draw renewed energy from its success....*

Helen A. Archdale
International Secretary

The clamor for Emily to be the first woman appointed to the Senate grew stronger each day. People in high places were also discussing it—not always with enthusiasm. Prime Minister Mackenzie King, for instance, while giving a political salute to the idea itself, was not wholly sympathetic to Emily as the first choice: "...as respects the appointment to the Senate of persons resident in provinces other than those in which the vacancies exist, I fear there are difficulties in the way which are unsurmountable..." William R. Howson, President of the Provincial Federal Liberal Executive, and an eminent Edmonton barrister, expressed his support for Emily's appointment in a two page letter to the Prime Minister and received, as Emily had, a similarly noncommittal reply.

Did Emily, as some have suggested, desperately want the appointment? I believe she did—and with every right. When it failed to materialize, she accepted the situation with grace—outwardly at least. In her correspondence, for instance, she alludes to the subject with a "May the best woman win" attitude, which she may have been far from feeling.

Appointed in 1930, Mrs. Cairine Reay Wilson was the first woman senator in Canada.[8] The Calgary *Herald* of March of that year was blunt:

> Premier King has given official endorsation to the view of the Privy Council that a woman is a "person" and therefore eligible to sit in the Canadian Senate, by appointing a member of the fair sex to that body. It cannot be said that the Prime Minister acted with undue haste in creating the precedent. He took several months to think it over, and his choice finally fell on a fellow citizen in Ottawa...It will be a matter of passing regret that the honour did not fall to a westerner. A group of Alberta women led the successful fight to assert the right of the sex to sit in the Senate. The lack of a vacancy precluded one of them being selected to lead the way into the Red Chamber....

In her inaugural speech, Mrs. Wilson said she owed her appointment to "...the bravery of the five pioneer women from the province of Alberta who took the plea for admission of women to the Senate, to the highest court..." While Senator Wilson did not "set the furze afire," she brought no discredit to the post either.

Alluding to the situation some years later, R.M. Harrison of the *Border Cities Star* observed that "Despite the noble efforts of Janey Canuck—peace to her ashes—politics is still a stag party." It would have been less so, I venture to suggest, with a Senator Murphy. As one minor government official put it when asked for his opinion as to why Mrs. Murphy had been passed over: "She'd have made too much trouble, of course!"

Senate reform has been a catchword throughout Canada's history as a nation, and (according to Anne Francis writing in the *Toronto Daily Star* in 1961) it was Emily Murphy who modernized the Upper House. As a result of her actions there have been many women senators who, "weight for age are more lively than the male," and who have done a great deal to stir the conscience of Canadians on matters of social welfare, prison reform, the plight of refugees and hungry children in other parts of the world. On all these issues they have voted as experienced persons rather than as women, the one notable exception being the episode in which four women senators on the committee studied capital punishment. Two of them voted in favor of abolition and two against. But Senator Iva Fallis voted against the bill to make the Supreme Court of Canada the final court of appeal. "I never could trust the Supreme Court," she said, "after it decided that women aren't persons."[9]

On the evening of June 11, 1938, Prime Minister King unveiled in the lobby of the Senate a bronze plaque, placed there by the Canadian Federation of Business and Professional Women's Clubs, to honor The Five. Nellie McClung, one of the two surviving members of the little group (the other was Irene Parlby), was in attendance.

Each year since 1979, there have been five awards given to five outstanding persons who have fought for sexual equality. The awards were created to commemorate the 50th Anniversary of The Persons Case of 1929. So far, women have been the only recipients, but if the true meaning of the word Person is to be commemorated, and the work of the five originators of its clarification is not to be in vain, it is hoped that men, too, will qualify. As Emily said, they did not fight for a sex victory, but rather to be able to say "we" instead of "you" in affairs of State.

Chapter IX

The Trumpets Sound: 1930-1933

We should proceed harmoniously and with directness to those matrimonial objectives that are so high and so eminently desirable.

In the wake of the successful outcome of the Persons Case, invitations to The Five to speak and write about their favorite topics quadrupled, and Emily took advantage of every new opportunity. She talked about the opening up of the North, about the havoc caused by Canada's lax immigration laws, particularly as they pertained to the Chinese, and about the need for equality of justice for the poor by providing a public defender, instead of the accused person providing his or her own counsel.

"What is wrong with marriage?" she asked, attacking the new sexual freedom that was responsible for rising divorce rates, and answered herself: "People who enter into it are uncouth, ungentle persons who break their obligations as well as the heads and hearts of their bounden partners."

She wrote about the war she dreaded was coming. In "Do Women Oppose War?" (*Canadian Home Journal,* November 1930) she recounted a tea-table conversation which took place at a convention she attended in Banff. The question was a provocative one: were women as equally infected by war hysteria as men, or did they submit to it out of sheer apathy?

"All this talk about the end of war being brought about by the influence of women in parliament," says 'the Colonel,' her protagonist, "is the merest poppycock. It is my opinion, Madam," he goes on, "that in the cause of peace your sex will always remain unmoved and inactive, even as now—that, for the most part, they must inevitably be classified as shirkers of peace." The Colonel was prodding—very eloquently too—and Emily, along with other women at the table listened, for something told them they were hearing truths. A journalist at the table joined in: "You see, Madame," he said, "women are preached, sung and written into the war mood just the same as men, and are quite as amenable to propaganda, slogans and half truths."

Very skilfully in her article, Emily wove the conversation and the women's attempts (most of them futile) to rebut the Colonel's forceful argument, into a call for more positive action on the part of women to work for peace before it was, once more, too late. Much of what was said at that table in Banff has relevance today, particularly the Colonel's remarks that

...The preparation which America is making for war today is without a parallel in the world's history. Their annual budget is...higher than that of any of the so-called military nations of the world...They endorsed a treaty renouncing war and then, almost immediately, passed a naval bill which provided for fifteen warships...Twenty-one million American women have been led into a quiescent attitude by what the propagandists said concerning the necessity for what they described as "parity."

And he reminded them of the old song about the relative sea power of Britain and Germany:

> The Kaiser built another ship
> And Johnny Bull two more;
> The Kaiser then two others built
> And Johnny Bull built four.
> The Kaiser then four others built
> And so on o'er and o'er,
> Which left them both as you can see
> Right where they were before.

One may ask if men had continued to so delude themselves on the subject of war, could women effectively alter the course of history? Even Emily was at a loss for an answer. She above all realized that, despite the gains that women had made, they still had a long way to go. As the war drums began their first distant roll in Europe, she wrote to a friend, in July of 1931, "I'd like to go to Geneva, on that Committee which goes in February to discuss disarmament. I am conceited enough to think that I have written more on the subject in Canada than anyone else and have completer files. I was also Convenor of Peace and Arbitration for the National Council of Women of Canada and for a time a member of the General Committee of the League of Nations. There is no use in my even hinting it though, for no mere woman would have any chance whatever."

There would have to be a fundamental change in the attitudes of women, Emily believed, before equal status with men could be achieved:

> Women often lack initiative. They are afraid to launch out. That little experiment of Christopher Columbus cost $7,000. It was a good thing he had the nerve to try it. Every new continent of achievement lies overseas. Many persons fear to undertake projects which they might easily perform, because they cannot see the end of them. They forget that at every point the question settles itself when all the facts are considered. By attaining one step the next becomes clear...The progressive woman goes about her work with the spirit of an athlete. She delves into it, not because it is required of her, but to gain power to do it better. This is the normal impetus

of the progressive mind. It is a great day in a girl's life when she begins to discover herself. The latent capacity in each of us is greater than we realize, and we may find it if we search diligently. Women ought to be more impatient. There is no virtue in sitting quietly by, accepting the slow processes of the evolution of an idea.

Emily did not think "the progressive mind" had to reject more traditional values. Once asked what she considered woman's greatest gift to be, she unhesitatingly responded: "Motherhood."

In September 1931, on a visit to Toronto, Emily sat, by request, for a portrait by J.W.L. Forster, O.S.A., which was destined, according to the *Edmonton Bulletin* of May the following year, "for a national collection."[1] In doing so, she joined other famous sitters, including Pauline Johnson, Bliss Carman, Archibald Lampman, Charles G.D. Roberts, and Archbishop Stringer. A portrait of Louise McKinney, also by Forster, hangs in the legislative buildings in Edmonton. Forster painted many famous people, among them Queen Victoria on the occasion of her jubilee, the Emperor and Empress of Japan, and William Lyon Mackenzie.

In her portrait Emily is shown wearing a gown of fine Italian lace in ivory, and draped on her shoulders is a black and gold Venetian shawl. On one shoulder she wears her decoration of Lady of Grace of the Order of St. John of Jerusalem. "One feels," said the *Bulletin*, "that the artist has caught the writer and the visionary, the woman who places her fingers on the pulse of Canada and reveals to readers in many lands what she discovers. Here is the real spirit that has made Emily Murphy a world figure and a fighter for reforms, with an everlasting faith in human nature, for lo, these many years."

On November 21, 1931, Emily retired from the bench. She was sixty-three. In her letter of resignation to the Attorney General of Alberta she wrote:

Having served fifteen years as stipendiary magistrate in and for the City of Edmonton, and having passed the age period for retiring, it is now my desire to resign from this position.

If it meets with your approval, I still desire to remain a police magistrate and judge of the juvenile court in and for Alberta, my services being available for relief work, or for any special duties such as you might require, either in the courts or in institutional supervision.

It is with deep regret that I feel obliged to take this step, having been deeply interested in my work and in its various phases and having always received the utmost consideration from yourself and your predecessors in office.

It is my desire, however, to finish a very considerable amount of literary work which is only partially written, and also to give a more personal attention to my own business affairs.

The J.W.L. Forster portrait of Emily Murphy

To a friend she confided: "I promised the family I would retire when I had served fifteen years. There is so much work piled high on the table in my study, that I have to work at another table!"

Emily's resignation was accepted with regret, and she left many a moist eye behind her on the day she departed. Over the years she had become a much admired figure around the police courts, and although undoubtedly there were those who said she had her faults, as she would have been the first to admit, she had brought a humanity and compassion to her work that was new. The police, the clerks, the bailiffs, librarians, reporters, and even the lawyers had come to like and respect her. Her colorful personality, occasional ripe phrase, and booming laugh had lightened many an otherwise dull day, as it did when she was accused once of swaggering into court. "Oho!" she boomed. "Better to swagger than to stagger."

Although there is no record of any "retirement party," there must have been one, when old memories and past happenings were trotted out and laughed over with warmth and fond remembrance—like the time when Emily, asked by a rather patronizing interviewer, what other offices she had held, completely bewildered him by saying she had operated a furnace, a sewing machine, a foreign servant, a typewriter, organ, timber-limits, church bells, farms, coal mines, Ford car and a Colt gun. She had preached sermons, marketed grain, planted gardens, cooked thousands of dinners, painted pictures and broken broncos. Her clerks, who were there at the time, never tired of relating that story.

Then there was the case of the two lovelorn Arabs whose intended brides, arriving in Canada for the wedding with a retinue of brothers and sisters, were refused admittance by immigration officials when one of the brothers was found to have an eye infection. The voluble protestations of the future bridegrooms were cut short when a rival vowed death and vengeance upon them, and although it was not clear whether the rival intended marrying one or both of the young ladies, the ensuing furor spilled over into the press, and the matter was laid before Emily for solution. (MAGISTRATE MURPHY HEARS LOVERS SIGH, SHEIKS GROWL.)[2] Emily ordered police protection for the brothers and one presumes things ended happily ever after.

Emily was not a proud person as a rule, but there was one thing she was never loath to talk about: on the subject of her office filing system she bragged unmercifully. On one Civic Holiday, when she was entertaining some visitors in her office, Arthur and Evelyn joined the group, knowing full well it would not be long before the filing system would be produced for inspection. Despite the murderous looks they got from Emily, the two of them put it to a rigorous test, and had to admit it was all it was cracked up to be.

Emily had just two more years left to her. She might have had a premonition of death because her bouts of illness were becoming more frequent and severe. In September of 1932, she confided to Bill Deacon: "The Women's Business Club of Canada have inaugurated a movement to put a table in the Hall of Fame at Ottawa to this poor creature, and to my association in the Persons matter. Should they succeed and should they invite me to the unveiling, I might go, although it might be an embarrassing position. One might have a kind of "caught in the act" feeling. Anyway, it will probably be a long way off, by which time I can look over the Palisades of Paradise and observe it all from a safe distance."

In December of 1932, just ten months before she died, she wrote a "farewell letter" to the family. It was found in her safety deposit box.

In what remaining time she had, Emily lived her life to the fullest. In September of 1933 she gave Bill Deacon an account of how she almost got arrested for causing a nuisance at some protest gathering or other: "Almost got cracked on the head at the last unlawful assembly in our city market place, as a Mountie who had lifted his baton to fetch me 'one' on the head suddenly lowered it with discretion, saluted and apologized. See how I missed becoming famous...for it was plainly the officer's duty to try out the thickness of my skull as he did that of a barrister standing close by. Living in interesting times are we not, William?"

Emily, a year before her death, 1932

On an October morning in 1933, Emily dressed and went downtown full of high spirits. She planned to stop in at the public library to research some material for an article she was writing, and maybe stay downtown for a bite of lunch. On the way she decided to drop in at the police court for a visit with some of her old cronies.

She arrived in time for the hearing of the last case before the noon adjournment, and when it was over sat chatting for a few minutes with Judge George McLeod and prosecutor Charles Becker. "The acoustics in this court are awful," she remarked. "It is very hard to hear anything." Colonel McLeod, turning to Eardley Jackson, defence counsel and veteran court strategist (who had been responsible for many a drama in Emily's court), asked him to go up to the Bench and speak, while Emily, he and two newspapermen, listened in at the rear.

Mr. Jackson walked to the magisterial dais and then, at Emily's urging, to the Bench. At a nod of approval from Colonel McLeod, "Magistrate" Jackson took his seat, folded his hands, cleared his throat and, assuming the dignified pose of a jurist, said: "Ladies and Gentlemen, we are honoured today by the presence of Mrs. Emily Murphy, Police Magistrate and Judge. A feminine note missing from this building...is brought back by the kindly, smiling countenance of this beloved lady." This from Emily's sworn enemy, the man who seventeen years before had so blatantly called into question her right to preside in court because she was not a "person," the man who had plagued her with objections at every opportunity for months afterwards.

The impromptu speech caught everyone by surprise. There was silence for a moment afterwards, and then a burst of approving applause. "Thank you, Mr. Jackson, that was sweet of you," smiled Emily, as she left with Colonel McLeod and prosecutor Becker for lunch in the Judges' private chambers.

During lunch Emily realized she had left her eyeglasses at home. No sense going to the library without them, so she phoned Evelyn who hopped in the car and brought them to her. They did a little window shopping, with Emily remembering she needed some linen thread, of which—to Evelyn's amusement—she bought three large spools, "just to have plenty around." "After all," as she would often say, when her well-known predilection for wholesale quantities was under fire, "My father always bought everything by the barrel, and I'm my father's daughter."

Emily was a little longer at the library than she had expected, but she was home by streetcar about five o'clock. Supper with Evelyn and Arthur was the usual jolly time of chit chat about events of the day, after which the women retired to read the papers and Arthur went off with his friend, the Bishop of Edmonton, to watch women's basketball. (The Edmonton Grads were playing the Chicago Red Devils.)

Emily saw him to the door, joking about how young he looked, as he kissed her goodbye.

Arthur never saw her alive again. When he returned, he did not disturb her as she had already gone to bed and to sleep, after applying cold cream to her face ("I'm not going to let myself get old and wrinkled"), writing a few letters and learning to her satisfaction that the Edmonton team was winning.

Evelyn had just turned out her own light a little after midnight, when she heard a short cry from her mother's room. Within seconds she was there, but it was already too late. Emily had died in her sleep, "Like one who wraps the drapery of his couch about him and lies down to pleasant dreams."[3]

In response to Arthur's frantic phone calls, three doctors arrived shortly and announced that death was due to cerebral emboli, with diabetes a contributing cause. The date was October 26, 1933. Kathleen was already at her mother's bedside when the doctors arrived.

Stark disbelief lined their faces as husband and daughters gazed at one another. Everything had seemed so normal, so happy, so usual. There had been no inkling of impending tragedy. A family friend, a yachtsman, on hearing the sad news from Evelyn, said "There was something very gay and gallant about your mother, and I like to think that all other good skippers dipped their flags in her honour the night she brought her vessel home. 'So she passed over, and all the trumpets sounded for her on the other side.' "

Evelyn broke the news to her mother's great friend Bill Deacon in a letter which she concluded by saying: "...I wanted you to know how happy and free from care or foreboding was her passing. It's as she would have wished, but it's black, black hell for those of us left behind, knowing there was no time to tell her how we loved her. I guess though that she never was under any doubt or delusion about that for, being Irish, we never hid our 'more tenderer feelings' from each other, and no movie actress ever got so many enthusiastic hugs in her lifetime as Mother got from Dad and Kathleen and I in a week."

Bill Deacon was devastated. He was one of the first to pay tribute, and the Toronto *Mail and Empire* of Saturday, November 4, carried a glowing valediction to his old and dear friend.

> I hate speaking publicly out of an acute personal grief, but Emily Murphy...stood by me in life, [and] I must stand by her in death and indicate, as best I can, what that wonderful woman was like. She was a millionaire of the heart and the mind...After absence, she would greet an old friend with a boom of welcome that reminded me of the salute of a friendly battleship. She was quite short and stout, and walked with the lusty, sea-going roll of a sailor ashore...We must have made a queer pair walking up the streets of Winnipeg, I so tall and thin, she so short and stocky. If a sidewalk jam separated us I could still see her over the heads of the crowd and still hear her, for her voice would strengthen and the tale go on...That I admire her, and was fond of her, her quick intuition would tell her at once. But I was barely more than half her age and a young lawyer. She commanded my respect as a woman and a sitting judge...The self-reliant, resourceful spirit of the pioneers stirred her to the many activities for which she will be remembered in official history...she showed the women of Canada ...that the time has come for a new sort of pioneering: that the women must take hold of affairs, and use their minds, and make their wits felt, so that we can leave a better world than the man-made one into which we were born. Who will take up her challenge, follow her example? Many will, and do great things. Let them remember Emily Murphy, who blazed that broad trail to a nobler future...

Letters of condolence flowed in and tribute after tribute tumbled from the pages of the press. After Deacon, Lotta Dempsey, Emily's young reporter friend, remembered her "overwhelming kindliness," and her "swift encouragement for those who struggled."[4]

Nellie McClung praised Emily's "burning love of justice, a passionate desire to protect the weak, and to bring to naught the designs of evil persons."

"Mrs. Murphy," she added, "loved a fight and, so far as I know, never turned her back on one."[5]

Prime Minister R. B. Bennett, who had swept the Depression-ridden country in the election of 1930 on the promise to "blast a way into the markets of the world...and end unemployment or perish in the attempt," sent a letter of condolence on the loss of "A greatly beloved friend."[6]

There were letters to the editor from people who had known Emily, if only in passing. Each of them recalled some special quality about her which had made the meeting a memorable one. "She was always willing to go the extra mile," wrote one newspaper columnist, referring to the time when, en route to the hospital for an eye operation, he had met Emily. She visited him the next day with candy, oranges and bright chatter.

Inevitably, there were pontifical utterances from those who wished to be identified in some way with the woman who had captured the hearts and minds of so many. One anonymous scribe called her "A pioneer on the frontier of understanding of social responsibility in the 20th Century." Another declaimed: "[She had] in her eyes the look of the crusaders...those eager souls who see the hills delectable in the distance and are willing to take the wearying steps to reach them, who, even with their own clear vision, are willing to try to hold out their hands and help with them all those who are struggling to follow..."

Some time later, Emily was paid a generous tribute by the McLennan Chapter of the Imperial Order Daughters of the Empire, who, "Wishing to be known by the name of a woman who is representative of the finest in achievement for her sex," sought permission to become known as the Emily Murphy Chapter.

The funeral was held on Monday, October 30, with a service at the Holy Trinity Church officiated by the Bishop of Edmonton. Emily's coffin was carried by several of "her" policemen, brother Gowan, and son-in-law Cleave Kenwood, for burial in Edmonton Cemetery Mausoleum. People from all walks of life came by the hundreds to pay their last respects. Two of Emily's "fallen women" shyly produced a rose, and with a sudden burst of courage placed it in the casket before the lid was closed. It was not removed; the family knew Emily would have wanted it that way.

There were no sittings at the Police Court that Monday afternoon.

Many years later, Emily was honored by the National Historic Sites and Monuments Board by being designated "A person of national historic importance." It was the Board's highest rating, and placed Emily equal in rank with Sir Wilfrid Laurier and Samuel de Champlain. The City of Edmonton gave her name to a new twenty-seven-acre park on the south bank of the North Saskatchewan River. Most recently, the house at 11011-88th Avenue, where Emily had lived with her family for fourteen years, was declared a historic site.

Emily was survived by Arthur, her two daughters, sister Annie, brother Gowan and grandchild Emily.

Kathleen, Arthur and Evelyn in 1933

Arthur was inconsolable for months after Emily's death. He eventually moved to Vancouver, where he could play his beloved golf all year round. Then seventy-seven, he was to live another sixteen years. He continued driving his car until he was ninety, and only gave up hunting when in his eighties "because I'm getting a bit shaky." When asked what his recipe for longevity was, he once said, "Nine months of golf, two months of shooting, one month loafing, and a bit of preaching on the side."

Arthur was often asked about his thoughts on life and, philosopher that he was, usually had an answer. "I don't think that life can die," he said, "and I'm optimistic enough to look forward with great pleasure to the first fifteen minutes after they say I'm dead." Or: "It is in the next world that the really great things will be accomplished. I've no use for a man who's not greater than a creed. The man's the thing."

Nellie McClung, one of Emily's closest friends, a fellow author, and fighter, paid tribute in a letter:[7]

Arthur Murphy in 1934

My dearest Evelyn,

I cannot yet grasp just what we have lost, but I know the whole world is poorer. And yet we must not forget to be thankful that this bright soul so gallant and courageous and altogether lovely, stayed on earth and enriched it for these years. And tho' her going, so suddenly, has left us dazed and stunned, it was a lovely way to pass from the light of earth to the glory of heaven. I know it is the way she would have chosen, but she, who loved life so well, would have gladly lived out her days.

Sometimes in school, a very industrious pupil, who has excelled the others, is allowed to quit at noon. So it has been with her.

Dear Evelyn, I hope you will take comfort in the knowledge that you did everything for your dear mother that a loving daughter could do. You were more than a daughter, you were a devoted companion, and adviser to her. You made her laugh, and by your delightfully human way of looking at life, kept the sorrows and sins of life from overflowing her, in the years she presided in the Police Court. It was a grim and terrible business to be facing wrongdoers each day, but when she came home she could shed the grayness of it as she changed her clothes, as you were at home, and the hearth fires were burning and the home was full of light, and cheerful conversation, and when she came down to dinner, in the atmosphere of peace and comfort, her strength was renewed. She often spoke of this to me. How she craved sweet odours, a dainty handkerchief, pretty slippers, colour and beauty to let her forget the seamy, sordid things of the day.

I couldn't put words together yesterday...I had only one feeling and that was desolation.

But life goes on, and we have to go with it. I know how brave and steady you are, dear Evelyn, and I want to tell you we all love you and are sending you our tenderest thoughts, and to dear Kathleen too.

Ever your friend,
Nellie L. McClung

So an enduring friendship passed into history, and an adored wife and mother took her leave. Emily Murphy had blazed a trail. It would now be up to others, encouraged by her example, to forge on as she had done, urging an acceptance of new ideas, righting the wrongs of the past. She had loved the fight, been bloodied in battle, and only when a deadly disease struck her down had she given up.

She had come, over the years, to love the West. Her first sight of Banff, Alberta, had inspired in her both eloquence and silence. "I hope to be transformed into a pine tree when I die...Words fail me." But Emily Murphy never forgot the land of her birth, Ontario, and perhaps the quotation she uses in the first chapter of *Janey Canuck in the West* will make a fitting epitaph for the close of this one...

When I forget thee,
Land of desire,
My hands shall be folded
And my feet not tire.

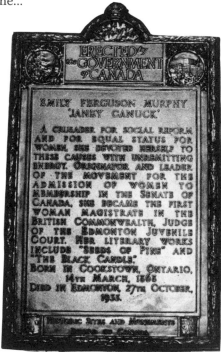

The plaque in Emily Murphy Park, Edmonton

Appendix I

Books by Emily Murphy

Impressions of Janey Canuck Abroad. London, Ont.: C.P. Heal, 1901.

Janey Canuck in the West. New York: Cassell & Co., 1910, Repr. Toronto: McClelland & Stewart, 1975.

Open Trails. New York: Cassell & Co., 1912. Repr. London: J.M. Dent, 1920.

Seeds of Pine. Toronto: Hodder & Stoughton, 1914. Repr. Toronto: Musson Book Company, 1922.

The Black Candle. Toronto: Thomas Allen, 1922.

Our Little Canadian Cousin of the Great North West. Boston: Page & Company, 1923.

Bishop Bompas. Toronto: Ryerson Press (Canadian History Readers series), 1929.

Appendix II

Excerpt from *Our Little Canadian Cousin of the Great North West*

So far as is known, *Our Little Canadian Cousin of the Great North West* is the only children's book Emily ever wrote. It was published in May, 1923, by a firm in Boston, Mass., and nothing very much more is known about it. It is an account for young minds of the traditions and history of the Canadian West, written in story form, without pretension and from a Canadian point of view. As an introduction to Canada this little volume succeeds quite well:

> The three Provinces of North West Canada referred to in this volume are Manitoba, Saskatchewan and Alberta. These include an area of 862,972 square miles and originally formed a part of Rupert's Land.
>
> In 1670, Charles II of England granted to certain traders a charter of incorporation to "The Governor and Company of Adventurers of England, trading into Hudson Bay." To these traders, this gave not only a monopoly, but a proprietorship of all the region drained by the rivers flowing into Hudson Bay. In return, the traders were required annually to give the King, or his heirs, two black beavers and two elks as an acknowledgment of his suzerainty.
>
> The motto of this trading company was *Pro Pelle cutem*, "A skin for a skin."
>
> Two hundred years later, in 1870, the Province of Manitoba was created from land bought by the Canadian Government of this Hudson's Bay Company and, in the year 1905, Alberta and Saskatchewan were also constituted to be Provinces.
>
> These three wide and wonderful Provinces combine a great variety of scenery and wealth of resources, and have drawn from all countries in the world for their population. This Canadian North West may be truly called "The Child of the Nations," embracing among its citizens—as it does—some thirty different nationalities.
>
> The original inhabitants, the Indians, were divided into different tribes, but by reason of their inter-tribal warfare, became greatly decreased in numbers. When the buffalo disappeared with the coming of the white man, the Indians were still further decimated, the remnants of the tribes now living on Indian reserves under the care of government agents.
>
> Great transcontinental railways have opened this enormous area to the world, so that our little Canadian cousins of these great Provinces are not so isolated as they used to be, and may now enjoy the same privileges as their cousins of Ontario, Quebec, British Columbia, and the Maritime Provinces. It is of these privileges, with the history, sport and home life of the country that we would talk....

Notes and References

Prologue—"To Hell with Women Magistrates"

1. Magisterial Correspondence, Edmonton City Archives.
2. The 1876 enactment that "Women are persons in matters of pains and penalties, but are not persons in matters of rights and privileges," came about when a woman in England, who knew that certain women once had the privilege of voting, since taken away, decided to vote and see what would happen. On election night she beguiled a poll clerk into giving her a ballot and voted. She was arrested and tried. The case—Chorlton *vs* Lings—produced the infamous ruling.
3. Alberta Law Reports 321-338, *Rex* v. *Cyr*.

Chapter I—Growing up in Cookstown: 1868-1882

1. Thomas Pakenham, *The Year of Liberty* (Toronto: Hodder & Stoughton, 1969), p.144.
2. Byrne Hope Sanders, *Emily Murphy: Crusader* (Toronto: Macmillan, 1945), p.4.
3. Deacon Collection, Thomas Fisher Rare Books Library, University of Toronto.
4. Wealthy Uncle 'Miah was the bachelor brother of Emily's father, who lived close to their home with "Granny Bryson and Old Barney," two servants who had come from Ireland with the family and stayed with 'Miah until they died. Despite his earthy language, 'Miah was a soft hearted man and an easy touch for impecunious nieces and nephews.

Chapter II—From Boarding School to Rector's Wife: 1883-1897

1. Byrne Hope Sanders, *Emily Murphy: Crusader* (Toronto: MacMillan, 1945) p.21.
2. Rare Books Library, University of Waterloo.
3. Emily Murphy, *Open Trails* (New York: Cassell & Co., 1910; Toronto: McClelland & Stewart, 1975), p.177.
4. *Ibid.*
5. *Ibid,* p.179.
6. *See* William B. Hamilton, *The Macmillan Book of Canadian Place Names* (Toronto: Macmillan, 1978).
7. No record of this meeting has come down to us, but among Emily's papers is a printed leaflet bearing McIntyre's picture.
8. Alexander Ross, "James McIntyre our Worst Poet Gets a Tribute" *Toronto Star* (September 22, 1972).

Chapter III—Impressions of Janey Canuck Abroad: 1898-1900

1. John Malcolm Brinnin, *The Sway of the Grand Saloon* (New York: Delacorte Press, 1971), p.226.
2. Frank E. Dodman, *Ships of the Cunard* (London: Adlard Coles, 1955), p.45.
3. For a full description of steerage conditions in the late 19th Century, see John Maxtone-Graham, *The Only Way to Cross* (New York: Macmillan, 1972).
4. The original Temple Bar was destroyed in the Great Fire. The one Emily saw is actually the second replacement erected in 1880. The "effigy" she refers to is actually a dragon, or "griffin" as it is properly called.
5. See Virginia Woolf, *Great Men's Houses* (London: Hogarth Press, reissued 1982).
6. *Joseph endeavours to ward off Death's fatal dart.* (Artist: Roubiliac.) Lady Elizabeth Nightingale, wife of Joseph Gascoigne Nightingale, died in 1751. *See* Edward Carpenter, ed. *A House of Kings* (London: John Baker, 1966).

7. Officially Bad Homburg, a famous spa in West Germany, north of Frankfurt in Hesse.

8. Dragon's Blood, according to Emily, is an enchanted wine, produced at the Castle of the Drachenfels, where Siegfried slew the dragon and bathed himself in its blood that he might become invulnerable.

Chapter IV—Dangerous Places: 1900-1903

1. Emily's nostalgic reference to "The old house where we lived [having] long since been destroyed by fire" (*Open Trails*, New York: Cassell & Co., p.226) was thought at one time to refer to the Ferguson family homestead. It is now known that the reference was to the home of Lt. Col. Thomas Roberts Ferguson, her uncle, ("Fighting Tom"). Her mother's move to Toronto was, indeed, to be closer to her family.

2. *The Globe and Mail*, "Toronto's Medical Health Office Marks Centenary" (March 14, 1983).

3. Charles Godfrey, M.D., *Rx Medicine for Ontario* (Belleville, Ont.: Mika Publishing, 1979).

4. Published as "Loose Leaves from the Diary of a Typhoid Patient" (*National Monthly,* November 1902).

Chapter V—Janey Canuck in the West: 1903-1907

1. The seeds roasted make a cocoa-like drink—ground, excellent cakes. Before blooming, if boiled, they taste like a cauliflower. The seed pods make blotting paper. The fibre of the stalk is useful and when dry is hard as maple. The seed heads, with seeds in, burn better than coal. The leaves can be used as tobacco. If planted in a malarial district they are a protection against fever. *See Janey Canuck in the West* (New York: Cassell & Co., 1910; Toronto McClelland & Stewart, 1975), p.13.

2. Nellie McClung, *Clearing in the West*, (Toronto: Thomas Allen, 1976), p.103.

3. Byrne Hope Sanders, *Emily Murphy: Crusader.* Toronto: Macmillan, 1945, p.88.

4. *No woman, idiot, lunatic or criminal shall vote.* (From the Election Act of the Dominion of Canada.) *See* Nellie McClung, *In Times Like These* (Toronto: University of Toronto Press, 1972), p.29.

Chapter VI—Edmonton: A New Life: 1907-1916

1. *See* J.G. MacGregor, *Edmonton, A History* (Edmonton: Hurtig, 1967).

2. This became 112th Street in 1914 when the city moved over to a completely numerical street system.

3. "She had no great sense of dress; she was unco-ordinated, flashy, wore vivid colours, often flamboyant with lots of bows and ribbons. She could be terribly hurt by criticism." (Lotta Dempsey, Emily's reporter friend).

4. For a complete list of Emily's achievements, see *Who's Who*, or *Emily Murphy: Crusader* (Toronto: Macmillan, 1945), by Byrne Hope Sanders.

5. From a radio address over CBR Vancouver, February 11, 1946, by Byrne Hope Sanders (University of Waterloo Archives).

6. *Emily Murphy, Crusader,* pp.108-110.

7. Emily Murphy, *Seeds of Pine* (Toronto: Hodder & Stoughton, 1914), p.187.

8. *See* Josephine Kamm, *The Story of Mrs. Pankhurst* (London: Methuen, 1961).

9. "The Cat and Mouse Bill" ended the forcible feeding of hunger strikers. Under it, hunger strikers were released once they reached the starvation point. The police would then watch their every move and usually re-arrest them before they regained their health.

10. Edmonton City Archives

11. In "What Janey Thinks of Nellie" (*Maclean's*, Sept. 1, 1921) Emily refers to her tour with Emmeline Pankhurst in Southern Alberta that same year, and alludes to her having learned solitaire then. Emily's memory is at fault here, or she used a literary expedient, for she records playing the game during her illness in 1913, in what must have been a later reprint of *Open Trails* which was first published 1912.

12. *See* Michael Bliss, *The Discovery of Insulin* (Toronto: McClelland & Stewart, 1982).

13. *See* Candace Savage, *Our Nell* (Saskatoon: Prairie Books, 1979).

14. A highly prized British decoration usually presented by the reigning monarch; there is no record that Emily travelled to Britain to receive hers.

Chapter VII—*The Black Candle*: 1916-1926

1. During 1916 and 1917, as a war policy, Alberta was "dry." After the war, prohibition continued, with occasional relapses, until liquor was placed under government control in 1924.

2. Recipe for Emily's Date and Nut Loaf:
   4 c flour
   4 tsp baking powder
   1 c white sugar
   1 c chopped walnuts
   1 c chopped dates
   1 egg well beaten
   2 c sweet milk
   pinch salt
Let rise 20 mins. Bake 1-1/2 hrs slowly. Makes 2 loaves. for one loaf use half and bake 3/4 hr. (*Edmonton Bulletin,* May 4, 1930).

3. "Magistrate Murphy Can Take a Good Joke" (*Edmonton Journal,* July 20, 1928).

4. Emily F. Murphy, "The Woman's Court," (*Maclean's,* Jan. 1920).

5. *Ibid.*

6. *Ibid.*

7. *Ibid.*

8. Byrne Hope Sanders, *Emily Murphy: Crusader* (Toronto: Macmillan, 1945), p.160.

9. *Ibid.*

10. For an account of trial see *Edmonton Bulletin* (May 13, 1924).

11. Emily's recommendations were: 1) Institutional (hospital) treatment to cure drug addiction to be available in every province; more severe penalties, with the option of a fine withdrawn. 2) All drugs to be procured from Government outlets, with a record kept of every grain from the moment it entered the country until it reached the ultimate consumer. 3) The practice of allowing physicians to prescribe large quantities of narcotics for their patients, to be administered by themselves, to be reviewed.

12. Michael Bliss, *The Discovery of Insulin* (Toronto: McClelland & Stewart, 1982), p.225.

Chapter VIII—Are Women Persons?: 1927-1929

1. Nellie McClung, *The Stream Runs Fast* (Toronto: Thomas Allen, 1945).

2. Alberta Women's Bureau, "Women are Persons": Centennial Bldg. 10015-103 Ave. Edmonton, Alta, 1979.

3. *See* Eleanor Harman, "Five Persons from Alberta" from *The Clear Spirit,* ed. Mary Quayle Innis (Toronto: University of Toronto Press, 1966), p.173.

4. Article by Nellie McClung, in the Toronto *Evening Telegram,* June 18, 1938, on the occasion of the unveiling of a memorial plaque in the Senate on June 11.

5. Emily Murphy, "The Case for Sterilization," *Winnipeg Tribune* (January 16, 1932).

6. C.B. Robertson, *Canadian Magazine* (September, 1929).

7. For a full account of the decision, its implications and political reactions, see the *Toronto Star* (October 18, 1929).

8. Mrs. Wilson was the wife of former Liberal M.P. Norman Wilson, and the daughter of the late Senator Robert MacKay, for many years one of the party stalwarts in the district of Montreal. She was also the founder of the Ottawa Women's Liberal Association and an officer of the National Federation of Liberal Women of Canada. Emily Murphy was a Conservative.

9. Anne Francis, "Does it Take a Woman to Reform the Senate?" *Toronto Daily Star* (July 18, 1961).

Chapter IX—The Trumpets Sound: 1930-1933

1. The Forster portrait of Emily Murphy is now in the Canadiana Collection of Toronto's Royal Ontario Museum.

2. *Edmonton Bulletin* (August, 1926).

3. Letter from Evelyn to William Arthur Deacon (Deacon collection, Robarts Library, University of Toronto).

4. *Edmonton Bulletin* (October 28, 1933).

5. *Edmonton Bulletin* (December 26, 1933).

6. Bennett had been a member of the Alberta Legislature and a staunch supporter, when Emily was fighting for her social reforms.

7. This letter is among private family papers.

Selected Bibliography

Bannerman, Jean. *Leading Ladies of Canada, 1639-1967.* Galt, Ont.: Highland Press, 1967.

Bonnycastle, Sir Richard. *The Canadas in 1841: Volumes I & II.* London: H. Coburn, 1841-2.

Francis, Anne. "Does it Take a Woman to Reform the Senate?" *Toronto Daily Star* (July 18, 1961).

Innis, Mary Quayle, ed. *The Clear Spirit: Twenty Canadian Women and their Times.* Toronto: University of Toronto Press, 1966.

James, Donna. *Emily Murphy.* Toronto: Fitzhenry & Whiteside, 1977.

Jones, Donald. "Religious Split 99 Years Ago Gave Birth to Wycliffe College." *Toronto Star* (May 5, 1976).

McClung, Nellie, *Clearing in the West.* Toronto: Thomas Allen, 1976; *In Times Like These.* Repr. Toronto: University of Toronto Press, 1972; *The Stream Runs Fast.* Toronto: Thomas Allen, 1945.

Nash, Helen A. "Dear Emily." *Canadian Red X Junior* (November 1958).

Sanders, Byrne Hope. *Emily Murphy: Crusader.* Toronto: Macmillan, 1945.

Thomas, Clara and Lennox, John. *William Arthur Deacon: A Canadian Literary Life.* Toronto: University of Toronto Press, 1982.

Index